I ♥ THE HAIRY BIKERS

THE HAIRY BIKERS'
COOKBOOK

Dave Myers and Si King

Additional material by John Stroud and Vikram Jayanti

MICHAEL JOSEPH an imprint of *Penguin Books*

DAVE: I would like to dedicate the book to the late Glen Howarth

SI: I would like to dedicate this book to my wife Jane and my three wonderful sons

MICHAEL JOSEPH

Published by the Penguin Group

Penguin Books Ltd, 80 Strand, London WC2R 0RL, England

Penguin Group (USA) Inc., 375 Hudson Street, New York, New York 10014, USA

Penguin Group (Canada), 90 Eglinton Avenue East, Suite 700, Toronto, Ontario, Canada M4P 2Y3 (a division of Pearson Penguin Canada Inc.)

Penguin Ireland, 25 St Stephen's Green, Dublin 2, Ireland (a division of Penguin Books Ltd)

Penguin Group (Australia), 250 Camberwell Road, Camberwell, Victoria 3124, Australia (a division of Pearson Australia Group Pty Ltd)

Penguin Books India Pvt Ltd, 11 Community Centre, Panchsheel Park, New Delhi – 110 017, India

Penguin Group (NZ), cnr Airborne and Rosedale Roads, Albany, Auckland 1310, New Zealand (a division of Pearson New Zealand Ltd)

Penguin Books (South Africa) (Pty) Ltd, 24 Sturdee Avenue, Rosebank, Johannesburg 2196, South Africa

Penguin Books Ltd, Registered Offices: 80 Strand, London WC2R 0RL, England

www.penguin.com

First published 2006

1

Copyright © David Myers and Simon King, 2006

Food photography copyright © Noel Murphy, 2006

Reportage photography copyright © Big Bear Films Ltd/VIXPIX Films Ltd and Chris Terry, 2006

Photographs taken on location by John Stroud, Vikram Jayanti, Belinda Morrison, Dave Rea, David Keene and Dave Depares

By arrangement with the BBC

BBC logo © BBC 1996

The BBC logo is a registered trade mark of the British Broadcasting Corporation and is used under licence.

The Hairy Bikers' Cookbook is a Big Bear Films and VIXPIX Films co-production.

The moral right of the authors has been asserted

Set in Clarendon and Nimbus Sans

Printed in Great Britain by Butler & Tanner Ltd, Frome, Somerset

A CIP catalogue record for this book is available from the British Library

ISBN-13: 978-0-718-14908-6
ISBN-10: 0-718-14908-4

INTRODUCTION

Over the past year, as we bumbled our way around the globe, certain questions kept resurfacing: Who's got the map? Where's me lemon zester? What's Portuguese/Romanian/Vietnamese for garlic? What time is it in Newcastle...? But on every trip, one question above all was bound to surface at some point. We'd look at each other with a mixture of panic and sheer pleasure, and ask, 'What the hell are we doing here?'

It's not an easy question to answer. Unlike a lot of TV shows, *The Hairy Bikers' Cookbook* grew out of our own lives, rather than being dreamt up in some executive's swanky office. For years, when a break from work came along, we'd been abandoning our loved ones in favour of a couple of weeks on the bikes, exploring weird and wonderful places and the fabulous food they offered. And the more trips we did, the more we wanted to go on doing them. After a while, Dave summed up the situation in his usual succinct manner: it was all very well travelling the world, stuffing our faces and talking bollocks, but would anyone actually pay us to do it?

We'd worked behind the scenes in television for years. In fact we'd met while working on one of those Catherine Cookson dramas (Dave was doing the make-up, and Si was working as a location manager, persuading Britain's minor aristocracy to hand over their country seats to a bunch of grumpy film technicians). With hindsight, there was a certain inevitability to us getting together: we both loved biking, cooking and... talking bollocks. Over the sale of a bike (which promptly blew up), a friendship was formed that has survived everything: Dave's brain tumour, Si's flatulence, and the wrath of Si's missus when we shaved the dog with a beard trimmer. But that's another story.

But working in television is not the same as being on television. In fact coming from one to the other is in some ways a distinct disadvantage: the industry is full of people who reckon they could do the presenter's job, and producers are understandably suspicious as a result. But at least we knew some people we could call, to try out our mad scheme. We'd both worked with a producer/director called John Stroud, and he loved the idea. But although he'd started out in documentaries, his company was better known for comedy and drama, so he called up an old mate, Vikram Jayanti.

Vikram was one of the people behind the brilliant documentary *When We Were Kings*, about Muhammad Ali's great fight in Zaire against George Foreman. Stroudie persuaded him to meet us for lunch, and apparently it was Si explaining how his mum's tongue-press worked that convinced him he wasn't dealing with a couple of normal wannabe presenters – that, or our description of how to make udder pie. He was intrigued, which is how eventually we came to be the only cookery show with an Oscar-winning producer.

We're not chefs, as we've always been at pains to point out. We don't have a string of restaurants and a talented staff to yell at, and we probably wouldn't enjoy it if we did. We're cooks, pure and simple. We love to cook, for mates, family, kids and each other. We don't agree about everything (Si's kids were once forced to adjudicate in a fearsome row over the best way to cook couscous), but we're both convinced of the importance of food as a kind of social glue. Food is the commonest of all currencies, the most universal of languages, and the more we've travelled, the more we've become aware of its importance. It's what gets us going in the morning, and what sends us to bed happy at night. And, in the case of Kingy's addiction to tripe, gets you up again shortly after that...

The adventure started in Portugal and it has been an adventure; at different times scary, ridiculous, knackering, astonishing, but always enormous fun. We've done some distance – about 1,200km off-road in Namibia alone – and we've eaten some of the most delicious food man has yet come up with (mind you, we've also eaten scorpions, mopane worms and a goat's penis, so that redresses the balance a bit). It turns out that the world is not a small place at all; it's massive and the more you dig into it, the more you find. This book just scratches the surface but what we've tried to get across is that wherever you are in the world – home or abroad – there are good ingredients to be found and new ways of cooking to be enjoyed, if you're prepared to try.

That's our motto: just give it a go...

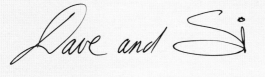

SANTANDER

PORTO

SPAIN

PORTUGAL

SANTARÉM

NAZARE

EVORA

FARO

Portugal

DAVE: For most people, there's one wonderful moment when a journey really begins. In fact, for an all-too-brief second it's more than that: it's the start of an adventure. It's that moment when the door of the plane swings outwards and, as you stumble blinking into the sunlight, a wall of heat hits you. And then the smell of tarmac, and aviation fuel, and maybe the sea...

What hit us as we rode across the border from Spain into Portugal was more like a bucket of cold water. It was late October, and out in the Atlantic the hurricane season had been barging around like a large wet dog in a small room – a dog whose big waggy tail was about to deposit several tons of water on two unsuitably dressed bikers. Don't get us wrong, we're used to rain – after all, we're bikers – but when it's running down the inside of your glasses, you know you're in trouble. By the time we reached Chaves, the first stop on our tour, we looked like two somewhat overfed kittens pulled out of a canal in a sack. Our director Stroudie, meanwhile, was still moaning about the lack of a proper sign at the border: 'How can you cross into a country without a "Welcome to Portugal" sign? That was going to be my opening shot.' Clearly the new Europe *sans frontières* was going to be a big disappointment to him.

When it came to setting up our first programme, we'd chosen Portugal as our first trip for a number of reasons. We're always drawn to countries that have a hidden, 'other' life that contradicts the usual image. Like a lot of people, when we thought of Portugal we thought mostly of the Algarve: golf-courses, pretty beaches, more golf-courses, and over-tanned expats complaining that their *Daily Telegraph* was a day late. Or perhaps we just thought of it as basically Spanish, bolted on to the side of Spain like a pannier on a bike.

How wrong we were. The Portugal that most of us see from our sun-lounger is a tiny corner of a much larger picture, a big country rightly proud of its own traditions and culture. It's the cork trees and heat hazes of the Alentejo, the massive breakers and mile-long beaches of the Atlantic coast, the bustle and noise of Porto, the vineyards and gorges of the Douro. And it's a really good ride...

But in Chaves, it was still raining. It rained all the way to the fumeria, where we tasted the wonderful smoked presunto ham, and dripped all over their spotless floors. And it hosed down even harder as we headed to Boticas, where a seventy-year-old man waited for us in rain that could flatten tin. Senhor Linhares and his wife were our first encounter with the friendliness and generosity of the Portuguese. Having gone to their cellar to learn about the 'wine of the dead', the tradition of burying wine in the ground to improve it, we were plied

not just with wine but sausage, presunto, home-made bread, brandy and fresh, dark honeycombs from their hives. As night fell, it was very hard to tear ourselves away.

Mr and Mrs Linhares were good examples of the people we met in Portugal: hard-working, traditional, generous, and very hospitable. The Portuguese jump at the opportunity to discuss food and wine, and go out of their way to repay your interest in their culture. Which did backfire on us a bit in Aveiro. We'd watched a lady called Maria gut tiny live eels with incredible dexterity, then fry them in beer with garlic and vinegar. And we'd tasted them. Well, to be honest, we'd tasted an awful lot, as they were delicious. This was unfortunate, because while Maria's entire family then tucked into a delicious-smelling feast of chicken cooked with chestnuts (see page 31), we were specially honoured with a huge bowl of . . . eel stew. Very good eel stew, made with saffron and wonderful Portuguese spuds; but you can have too much of a good thing, even eels. There was one great compensation, however. After dinner, Maria's son Umberto volunteered to take us to a fado club.

Fado has been described as a kind of Portuguese blues, but that doesn't really do it justice. It's a very emotional music, and when sung live it has an intensity that can make the hairs on the back of your neck stand up. We drove in a convoy with Umberto and his uncles deep into the countryside, until the sight of about fifty cars jammed into a narrow village betrayed the unlit presence of the club. The performers included an elderly man in an unlikely ginger suit (swiftly christened 'Papa Corduroy'), a young boy of about fourteen, and a beautiful dark-haired girl who melted our hearts. Well, mine anyway; Kingy was still marvelling at the musicianship of the guitarists who accompanied her. I tried asking her if she fancied a gig at the Roa Island Boat Club, but I don't think it came out quite right...

This could be because the owner of the club insisted on taking us down to his cellar to sample some real Portuguese hospitality. 'Don't try and shake his hand,' hissed Stroudie. 'Why not?' I asked, fearing some obscure breach of Portuguese etiquette. 'He hasn't got one,' came the reply. Didn't seem to stop him opening numerous bottles of wine with alarming alacrity. When we finally staggered back upstairs, we were met by Dash, one of the crew, looking ashen. 'I've pranged the Transit. Backed it into a car while I was trying to turn round.' We were sympathetic; there were a lot of cars crammed out there, and it could have been worse. Actually, it was: 'Um, it was our hire-car I backed it into...' We were glad we'd left the bikes back at Umberto's, otherwise he might have gone for the full set.

Bikes are great conversation-starters, especially when you're abroad. Alarm bells rang when we found a cop inspecting the Triumphs outside the fish market in Nazaré, until he showed us the bike tattooed on his hand and offered to be our unofficial guide for the day. This was fine, until he turned up in civvies on the beach and began a running commentary on our cooking abilities. When you're wrestling with a sea bass on a rickety picnic table in front of a film crew, you don't really need to hear how Silvio's mother's caldeirada is so much better than yours. Thanks, Silvio.

SI: We made it to the Algarve eventually, and after the wet and cold of the north it was great to feel the sun on our faces. Some of our gear even started to dry out a bit, although you could still have bred carp inside Dave's panniers. Perhaps that's what the smell was.

'Mr and Mrs Linhares were good examples of the people we met in Portugal: hard-working, traditional, generous, and very hospitable. The Portuguese jump at the opportunity to discuss food and wine, and go out of their way to repay your interest in their culture.'

Actually, the smell was probably the Portuguese water dogs we met. These web-footed creatures have been used since Roman times to herd fish into nets, and they're undeniably great dogs. They're also undeniably smelly; put together a thick, matted coat and a day spent plunging in and out of muddy estuaries and you get something you don't want curled up on your lap in front of the fire. But it was great to see them work . . . except they wouldn't. Wouldn't even go in the water. Too cold. We'd ridden through most of England, and then the length of the Iberian peninsula, and now the final day's filming was in jeopardy. But the owners had a great idea; they and the dogs jumped into Dave's inflatable dinghy (lugged all the way from Cumbria in the Transit), and motored out to the middle of the lagoon. Then they just chucked the dogs over the side.

Meanwhile, Dave and I were getting kitted up in our inflatable fishing suits, sort of rubber rings with waders and flippers attached. We drifted out into the lagoon, trying to look as if we were in control of the whole situation, and rapidly found ourselves being blown towards North Africa. 'Don't panic,' shouted Stroudie, arriving in the dinghy and panicking slightly, 'I'll tow you back.' Well, two big lads in giant rubber rings versus an inflatable dinghy with a tiny motor? No contest really – now all of us were heading for Morocco. 'Dave, I'll have to leave you behind. Don't worry, we'll be back soon,' said the director as he prised Dave's fingers off the grab-rail. The last thing I saw as we headed back to land was Dave's face bobbing about, yelling 'Bastards!' at the top of his voice. Then I lost sight of him, as the tears of laughter filled my eyes . . .

Filming usually ends each day with the phrase 'It's a wrap'; and the last day of filming ends with a wrap party. That night in Faro, once Dave had been towed out of the stagnant pool of cack into which he'd drifted, we had quite a party. We feasted in the local *churrasqueira* on steaks big enough for a small family to shelter under, then settled into a nearby bar. For rather a long time.

The next morning, we opened the Transit's doors to discover the parcel shelf and half the rear seat of the crew's hire-car. They'd been removed to give more room for filming on the move; no problem to stick them back in, except that the hire-car was by now on its way to Lisbon airport. What was really worrying was that Belinda, our brilliant line producer, drove 280km without noticing half the back seat was missing. Well, it was she who had insisted we drank caipirinhas all night; I'd have loved to have heard her explain that one to the hire company.

A few days later, we crossed the border back into Spain and headed north for the ferry at Santander. We were leaving behind a fascinating country and really friendly, hospitable people. 'No bloody sign again,' grumbled Stroudie, but it didn't really matter. We were on our way home.

BIKE BITS

OK, what's the low-down about riding in Portugal? Well, forgive the obvious but you've got to ride through Spain first, from Santander – that's the way we did it, anyway. Oh, another point: you ride on the right. Don't forget, 'cause it's gonna hurt if you get that one wrong.

We rode Triumphs in Portugal, Dave a Speedmaster and me a Bonneville America. We were both really chuffed to be on Triumphs and the bikes behaved well, albeit the Speedmaster had the edge on comfort over long distances (we completed 5,750km in 17 days) and was more agile around the mountain bends; the America tended to make hard work of it, unsurprisingly. We thought that both bikes could have done with a bit more bite at the top end and finished the journey wishing the engines had been 1000cc.

Road discipline in Portugal is OK, though not brilliant, so ride defensively. Portuguese drivers have a tendency to be erratic and bullish behind the wheel, an amalgam of Italian and German driving attitudes – not a good combination in our view. Taking this into account, we worked on the premise that the bigger the car the more aggressive the driver, a mantra that did not let us down.

The Portuguese roads are much better than they used to be, due to an influx of European money and an eagerness to keep them in good nick. Motorways are fast and safe, but the *estradas nacionais* (main roads) are picturesque and, for our money, offer the best in motorcycling, roadside cuisine and places to stay. Do watch out for roadworks; advance warnings are not of the standard found in the UK and normally involve a man in shorts with a red flag – or was it a man in red shorts and a flag? Either way, keep a weather eye.

Our outward-bound route was planned primarily to take in the sights, sounds and smells of an undiscovered Portugal, so our intention was to blast through Spain as quickly as possible (not the case on our return journey) to Bragança, then go to Chaves, Boticas, Porto, Aveiro, Mealhada, Nazaré, Santarem, Évora and finally Faro. This route gives a good flavour of the regional diversity of Portugal and what's on offer for bikers, foodies and travellers alike – oh, and some truly great roads whatever your ride.

Our homeward journey took in some of the best mountain roads in Spain. From León, we headed north to La Robla, then turned east towards the mountains on beautiful, fast country roads that slowly rise into some of the most awesome scenery. The N621 winds across stunning lakes and dams into alpine-style passes, where you're still likely to meet a herd of cows round the next corner. And there are great roadside truckers' cafés, with some of the best road-food to be found anywhere in the world.

The rain in Spain fell mainly on us! Coming back into Santander to catch the ferry home, we again hit rain of biblical proportions. Cars and trucks were aquaplaning across the carriageway and visibility was down to zero. Did we stop? No, we just kept riding; the bikes seemed OK, and we could see(ish). We couldn't get any wetter, so pulling over seemed a pointless exercise and we would have missed the ferry. It wasn't until we limped into the queue that we realised how lucky we had been. There had been several accidents and some nasty injuries to a couple of bikers. Bits of their bikes were being recovered from the road to put on the ferry; no one killed, thank God. The moral of the story is: leave yourself lots of time if the weather is dodgy; better to arrive early (or even late) than with bits of you and your bike missing.

FOOD BITS

When it was first mooted that we go to Portugal, we thought, what for? We're into motorbikes, not golf and bad sweaters covered in diamonds, and if we want sardines we can open a tin... But as with everything, you need to look a bit deeper and to examine the history to find the present. Portuguese explorers were hardly shy; in fact they were great, brave men who roamed the world. As a result, Portugal had a huge empire, and from there we can find the roots of modern Portuguese food.

It all began in 1419, when Henry the Navigator discovered Madeira, and then, in 1427, the Azores. His sailors ended up as far as the Cape Verde islands and Sierra Leone. However, in 1460 he died skint. Luckily for us, others took up the baton: in 1498 Vasco da Gama reached southern India, and in 1519–20 Magellan sailed around South America, paving the way for the colonisation of Brazil later that century. There were also Portuguese colonies in Japan and China, and their empire was for some time the largest in the world.

Now, when you come back from your jollies you bring back the local food for your chums. In Portugal's case it was a vast palette of new tastes: chillies from Brazil and Central America, spices from India and the Orient, sugar and other sweet treats from the Moors of North Africa. By comparison, all Sir Walter Raleigh brought back to England was spuds and fags – you see how a nation's culinary identity begins to present itself. The Portuguese also gave tips to other countries, taking tempura to Japan along with the habit of vinegaring the rice... or did the Japanese give that to the Portuguese? This is food anthropology – good, innit?

So the Portuguese food of today is a unique cuisine built on many traditions and five hundred years of practice. From the chillies of South America we get piri-piri; add some limes from Asia and a touch of booze from home. Result: bliss. Our beloved after-pub treat, the vindaloo, is also Portuguese, from their colony in Goa, the word a corruption of the Portuguese words for wine and garlic. Throw in a few chillies and vinegar and there it is, our gastric time bomb.

Some dishes depend more on tradition than, I feel, good taste. Take pork alentejo, for example... well, I wish someone would. It's a pork stew with clams or cockles, a kind of posh surf 'n' turf, and the locals love it. I had a rough one and it was like fishy stroganoff. The roots of the dish go back to the Spanish Inquisition, when it was used to catch out the Jews and Muslims. Refuse to eat it and you were on a fast track to the spiky chair.

And there are a lot of egg-yolky puddings in Portugal; the reason for this is the large number of nuns, who would use egg white to starch their wimples. This obviously created a few spare yolks to be made into rich puds, one famously being called 'nuns' tummies', another 'angels' breasts'. Even the Church had a saucy sweet tooth. There are a lot of almonds too. The story goes that a king in the Algarve was married to a Norwegian princess. She was homesick, so he planted the hillsides with almond trees so that in the spring it looked as though the hills were covered in snow. And quite apart from a happy Mrs there were a lot of almonds left over. By the way, try our cherry and almond tart; it would make any Viking grin.

In the north the pig is king; in Bragança there are prehistoric pig sculptures to prove it. Their soft and fragrant air-dried ham, presunto, is made from porkers fed on chestnuts and herbs. Try our trout de Bragança, where the fish is wrapped in it. Or you can visit Mealhada, the Las Vegas of the sucking-pig, where a whole town's economy depends on the consumption of piglets. Most locals also make their own chorizo sausage and it is so good. Portuguese bread and potatoes are also well worth a mention. The baking is unbelievable, as we found at Senhor Joao's bakery: loaves with ham and chorizo inside and little veal pasties that were so light they practically floated. So, yes, there is gastronomy in Portugal, and great wine, fish and port abound. All in the garden is rosy...Or is it?

One of the places the early explorers visited was Newfoundland, from where they brought back cod, salting and sun-drying their catch in order to do so. From this bacalhau was born. It's virtually the national dish of Portugal, with a huge following – but why? It was a perfect treat for the fish-loving but fridge-less folk in sixteenth-century Portugal; indeed one of its nicknames is 'fiel amigo', the faithful friend. Well, if I had a friend that smelled like that they would be out on their ear. It looks like a piece of pumice stone crossed with a flip-flop and it smells like a seagull's doormat. I know it's been around for years, but you can grow out of bad habits. We've all got fridges now and there is nothing better than a banging fresh piece of cod. Why bugger it up?

It is said there are 365 (although some say a thousand) ways of cooking bacalhau, one for every day of the year – and, yup, there is a special one for Christmas. You can have it as a rissole as part of your tapas (actually I quite like this with some cold beer), and a very popular dish is bacalhau with potatoes and olives, like a fish pie. Have it with chickpeas or with onions, with cream or with eggs in a kind of omelette. I tried it all ways up and I still don't like it but I know it's me versus a whole nation on this one and, luckily, there are lots of other lovely things to eat instead.

PORTUGUESE CHARCUTERIE
With Fig and Port Relish

We find that any charcuterie works well with this relish. Presunto ham is quite special as the pigs are fed on chestnuts and herbs, but Parma ham or Spanish serrano is also good, as is any spicy sausage or salami, and Spanish manchego cheese if you can't get Portuguese. And I particularly like the relish with bresola, the dried, cured beef. By 'eck, mother, the possibilities are endless!

Serves 4

for the relish
1kg of dried figs
250ml red wine
4 cloves
1 tspn black pepper
1 tbs white wine vinegar
250ml port
1 tspn sea salt
1 tbs extra virgin olive oil

to serve
presunto ham
chorizo sausage
slices of nice hard Portuguese
 mountain cheese
crusty bread

Soak the figs in the red wine for an hour or so. Then add the cloves, pepper and vinegar and cook gently until the mixture thickens. Add the port and salt, bring to the boil for two minutes and then allow to cool. Take half the mixture and blend with the olive oil until smooth, then mix with the remaining mixture so you have a relish with an interesting texture. This will keep for ages and is great with pork and lamb, as well as for tarting up a cheese sandwich.

Slice the ham, sausage and cheese thinly; serve with a generous dollop of the relish and some ace bread on the side.

CALDO VERDE

Caldo Verde is possibly the national dish of Portugal and we found the Portuguese to be among the greatest soup eaters on the planet. Ours is a twist on the traditional *Caldo Verde* with the addition of rich red spicy chorizo sausage.

Serves 8

You need a nice big pan for this!

1 small glass of port
2 nice fat onions, chopped fine
4 cloves garlic, crushed
4 tbs olive oil
6 big old potatoes, washed, peeled and diced

1½ litres good veggie or chicken stock
300g chorizo sausage chopped into small chunks
good big bunch of greens or cabbage
2 bay leaves
smoked paprika and olive oil for dressing
dense country bread to serve

First drink some port – it helps get you in the mood.

In your big pan, heat the oil, then sweat the onions and garlic for about 5 minutes until transparent. Add the sausage and carry on sweating like a Geordie in a spelling test. Add the diced spuds, which will absorb all the flavour from the sausage. Add the stock and bay leaves, season, then cook until the potatoes are soft – about 12–15 minutes.

Meanwhile, chop the greens or cabbage really fine – and I mean really fine; finer than a hummingbird's toenail clippings (or do what we did and go to the market and buy a cabbage-shredding machine made specifically for this purpose).

When the potatoes are ready, mash into the broth to make a thick chowder. In another pan, blanch the greens in boiling water for 1 minute to take off any bitterness, drain, then add as much to the simmering broth as it will support: if you want heavy soup add loads, if lighter, add less. Simmer for a few minutes.

Mix the smoked paprika with the olive oil, swirl this red magic into the vibrant green soup and serve to the crew with some heavy country bread and a smile. Wallow in praise.

TOMATO AND CHORIZO ACORDA

Acordas are soups thickened with bread, and, when they're made with seafood as a main course, are like culinary bran tubs as you dig through the soupy, bready loveliness to uncover prawns, clams and sometimes a lobster hiding in the bottom.

This one, however, is a yummy, comfy tomato and chorizo soup, inspired by when we were kids and used to soak bread in canned tomato soup until it was like a bowl of dough – how yummy was that! (We used to do it with fried cheese sandwiches, but this was a Bad Thing, and had to stop before we ended up like Elvis.)

This is nice with a little Parmesan or pecorino grated on the top. If you want it veggie just forget the meat. In Portugal it is traditional to poach eggs in the broth and then serve one to each person in their bowl. Eggy bread on your tomato soup…ooh, we could go on and on!

Serves 6

3 tbs olive oil
1 onion, peeled and sliced
6 cloves garlic, peeled and crushed
2 x 400g cans whole tomatoes, drained
1 tspn dried oregano
2 bay leaves
3 tbs flat-leaf parsley, chopped
1½ litres stock (veg. or chicken)

250g chorizo
250g belly pork
1 big loaf French bread
2 tbs fresh basil, chopped

to serve
grated Parmesan or pecorino
poached eggs (optional)

Heat the oil and sweat the onions and garlic for a few minutes. Add the tomatoes, oregano, bay leaves, parsley and stock, mush it all up and simmer for 15 minutes.

Meanwhile, chop the chorizo into small pieces and cut the belly pork into lardons. In a dry pan, fry the lot up until it goes slightly caramelised and crispy. Set aside.

Cut the crust off the loaf, tear the bread into small, ragged cubes and distribute it between the bowls. Add the meat and the basil to the broth and season to taste. Pour this over the bread and stir.

CHICKEN AND CHESTNUTS FROM AVEIRO

This is the dish that Umberto's mum cooked for the family whilst we tucked into our third helping of eels. It's lovely. The way the chestnuts take on the chicken juices makes this stew great. And it's just as great the next day, so don't worry about cooking too much.

Serves 6

2 medium free-range chickens	1kg chestnuts
1 carrot	4 tbs olive oil
1 stick of celery	1 head of garlic, peeled and chopped fine
1 onion, peeled and halved	(could be less if you like)
2 bay leaves	6 shallots, peeled and chopped fine
1 sprig of thyme	500g button mushrooms
12 black peppercorns	1 tbs cornflour
1 litre water	flat-leaf parsley, chopped, to garnish

First joint the chickens, then put the pieces in a big stock pan with the carrot, celery, onion, bay leaves, thyme, peppercorns and water. Simmer for about an hour or until the meat falls from the bones, periodically skimming off any scum that may rise. Allow to cool.

Whilst this is happening, put a cut in the bottom of each of the chestnuts and blanch them in boiling water for about 3 minutes to loosen their skins. Then plunge them into cold water and prepare for a fiddly time and a set of sore fingers as you peel them. Set them aside while you go back to your chooks.

Pick all the meat from the bones and strain off the remaining liquor. Set this aside.

Preheat your oven to 180°C. Meanwhile, heat the olive oil in a frying pan and sweat off the garlic and shallots, being careful not to scorch the garlic. When transparent, toss the button mushrooms in with them for about a minute.

Now assemble your stew. Put the shallot mixture in the bottom of a roasting tin, layer on the chicken pieces, then distribute the chestnuts evenly over the top. Add the liquor from the chicken but keep a cup back for later. Season to your taste, cover with foil and bake in the oven for about 30 minutes or until the chestnuts are soft. Don't overcook it or the chicken will go like Shredded Wheat.

At the end, mix the cornflour with the reserved cup of liquor, then add to the dish, stirring gently until it is thickened. Garnish with a sprinkling of parsley. This is great served with the vinegared rice and beans given over the page.

TROUT DE BRAGANÇA
With Vinegared Rice and Beans

You can use any kind of trout for this recipe (brook, brown or rainbow) but the more wild and organic the better. Some farmed trout are kept in conditions worse than the very worst battery-chicken farms.

Serves 4

the rice and beany bit
3 tbs olive oil
1 clove garlic, chopped fine
1 large onion, chopped fine
1 bay leaf
400g long-grain rice
1 litre water
1 can of red kidney beans, drained and rinsed
1 can white kidney (cannelini) beans, drained and rinsed
salt to taste
1 tbs white wine vinegar
$\frac{1}{2}$ tspn white pepper

the fishy part
4 small trout, gutted and cleaned (monkfish is a good substitute if you can't get trout)
250ml dry white wine
2 garlic cloves, sliced
2 bay leaves
75g plain flour
16 thin slices of presunto, prosciutto, Serrano or Parma ham
2–3 slugs of olive oil
100g unsalted butter
2 tbs lemon juice
a good handful of flat-leaf parsley, chopped

Marinate the fish for half an hour in the wine, garlic and bay leaves. While they are marinating, prepare the rice. In a big pan, heat the oil and sweat the garlic and onion, with the bay leaf, until transparent – about 5 minutes. Add the rice and sauté for 1 minute until it is nicely coated. Add the water, beans and salt, then cover and simmer until all the water has been absorbed and the rice is tender. Long-grain rice should take about 10 minutes, but if you're using something else, don't be shy: look on the back of the packet. Dress with the vinegar and white pepper, and a big knob of butter if you're feeling generous.

In the meantime, remove the fish from the marinade, reserving half a cup. Pat them dry with kitchen paper, sprinkle with black pepper, then dredge in the flour. Now, with the care of a midwife juggling babies, wrap the fish in the very thinly sliced ham, overlapping edges as you go. Think Egyptian mummies.

Heat the oil in a large frying pan, then add about half the butter and heat until it ripples. Reduce to a low heat and cook the fish for 2–3 minutes on each side until the ham is a golden brown, like crispy batter. Transfer to a warm plate. To the residue in the pan add the remaining butter, reserved marinade, lemon juice and parsley and boil hard for a couple of minutes until reduced by half. Pour this over the fish and serve with the rice and beans.

CALDEIRADA
or Portuguese Monster Fish-Stew Soup

For this, you need that really big pan again. Don't try to stick too hard to the fish listed here – be a bit inventive and, stopping short of a fisherman's wellie, use what you can get that is fresh and really good.

Serves 8

5 tbs olive oil

6 medium onions, finely chopped

8 cloves garlic, crushed

2 large green peppers, sliced

a good handful of flat-leaf parsley, chopped

as much saffron as you can afford

450g potatoes, peeled and sliced

2 or 3 bay leaves

12 peppercorns

4 large, juicy, ripe tomatoes, chopped (tinned are fine)

5 tbs tomato paste

700ml dry white wine

340ml water

squid

clams or cockles

900g oily fish such as mackerel, swordfish, or tuna

900g white fish like sea bass, monkfish, hake, or haddock

225g good, big raw prawns

2 dozen mussels

a handful of fresh coriander, chopped

to serve

good bread

piri-piri sauce

olive oil laced with truffle oil

Sweat off the onion, garlic and green peppers in the olive oil for about 10 minutes, nice and slow. Then cover to stew very gently for about 15 minutes – this is to knock down the green pepper into a more palatable form. Add the parsley, saffron, potatoes, bay leaves, peppercorns, tomatoes, tomato paste, wine and water, cover and simmer for 15 minutes. Then add the squid and clams and simmer for another 10 minutes. After this add the fish, prawns and mussels in layers. Don't stir; we want the fish to cook in the broth. Sprinkle with a heavy dose of black pepper, cover and cook for about 10 minutes or until the fish is cooked through and the mussels are open.

Ladle gently into vat-sized bowls and sprinkle with a chiffonade of coriander. It's bloody lovely: the aroma hits you like a hammer and your eyes will roll with glee. Serve with bread, and piri-piri sauce and olive oil for dipping.

PORTUGUESE CHERRY AND ALMOND TART

This is a real tart with a heart!

Serves 8

for the pastry

(to make about 280g, enough to line a 20cm (7½ inch) flan tin)

150g plain flour

30g icing sugar

80g chilled, unsalted butter

1 egg yolk, with a teaspoon set aside to glaze

for the filling

425g can of black cherries

2 tspns of ginginha, the Portuguese cherry brandy, or any other cherry brandy you can get

75g caster sugar

250g blanched almonds, about a third chopped chunky, the remainder medium/fine

zest of 1 lemon, finely chopped

zest of 1 small orange, finely chopped

1 cinnamon stick, ground

50ml port

125g unsalted butter

2 eggs

a handful of whole blanched almonds to finish

to serve

double cream or crème fraîche

First make the pastry, either by hand or in a processor. Sift together the flour and icing sugar, and rub in the butter to breadcrumb consistency. Add the egg yolk and mix until it forms a dough; if it's a bit too stiff, loosen with a very small amount of cold milk. Chill the pastry in the fridge for at least an hour.

Roll the pastry out thin and line the tart tin. Be gentle with her: she's a fragile old girl. Prick the base and leave to rest in the fridge for another half an hour. Preheat the oven to 180°C, then cover the pastry with parchment paper and baking beans, and bake for 20 minutes. Remove the paper, brush the beaten egg over the surface and put it back in the oven for about 5 minutes until it is shiny and lightly browned. Leave the oven on for the filling while the case cools on a rack.

Mash the cherries, de-stoning if necessary. Add the ginginha, which really is the best cherry brandy I have ever tasted – the heart of the tart – and then add sugar according to your taste. Spread evenly on the cooled tart shell. (Any leftovers can be a little treat with a dollop of ice cream – cook's perk.) Mix the chopped almonds, lemon and orange zests, cinnamon and port together and leave to infuse. Meanwhile, blend the butter and sugar, and beat in the eggs, then fold this into the almond mixture. Pour into the tart case and level off carefully, then arrange the whole almonds in a decorative shape on the top, to a design best left to yourself. Me, I'm a Virgo, so I prefer an orderly circular pattern; while Kingy, a Geordie, prefers 'rustic', i.e. he chucks them on as if he were pebble-dashing a council house. Bake in the oven for about 30 minutes or until the mixture has cooked through and your almonds are nicely toasted.

Serve with double cream or crème fraîche, whatever you prefer.

PURROS

NAMIBIA

WINDHOEK

SWAKOPMUND

BOTSWANA

SOUTH AFRICA

Sand

Namibia

DAVE: It had been a strange night. I'd woken once or twice in my tent but had been too knackered to worry about whatever it was that had disturbed me. We were on a recce with Paul van der Ploeg, a location manager and animal tracker, before the rest of the crew arrived in Namibia to start shooting. We'd driven into the bush in Paul's Land Rover and had made camp for the night. As we staggered into another glorious dawn, Paul was waiting for us with a cup of coffee. 'Hear anything in the night?' he asked. 'Something . . . dunno what. Why?' 'Have a look at this,' he grinned. And there, in the sand right outside my tent, was a great big paw-print. Of a lion.

That was the thing about this particular corner of Africa that we just hadn't got our heads around. When you head off into the bush in Namibia, you're not going into a game reserve to have a look at the animals; you're going into a completely wild environment, and they're coming to have a look at you. On the 1,200km that we did off-road during our filming trip, we saw one fence. So our close encounter with a lion should not have been so unexpected.

Paul assured us that a lion would be highly unlikely to attack us inside a tent. The only incident he could recall was when a tiny Japanese lady he was escorting on safari became aware of something poking the side of her tent. Next time it happened, she punched it as hard as she could, with the result that a very large and terrified lioness leapt several feet into the air and came down on top of the tent. That, in Paul's typically understated description, had taken a bit of sorting out.

Touchdown at Windhoek International airport is the first eye-opener. Out of one side of the plane you see the normal arrangement of sheds and hangars, and a white, low-built terminal building. Out of the other side of the plane you can see . . . well, bugger all really. Just mile after mile of bush stretching away across the plain towards the dark outline of distant mountains. 'It looks . . . big,' said Si, with his usual talent for stating the bleedin' obvious. He wasn't wrong, though; Namibia turned out to be a massive, empty, exhilarating challenge.

SI: We based ourselves in Swakopmund, a strange Germanic resort that seemed about as African as a pair of lederhosen. It has streets named after Bismarck and Kaiser Wilhelm, Black Forest gâteau in the cafés and (rather more worryingly) dodgy LPs of Goebbels' speeches in the antique shops. However, it also had two big bonuses: the excellent Tafel beer (and with the brewery in town, plenty of it) and a great bunch of people at Namib Film, who were busy setting up the expedition. Looking at the amount of tents, fuel, food, water and beer needed to take a thirsty crew on a fourteen-day shoot was a shock. This wasn't going to be like any trip we'd done before.

The best thing about Swakopmund (apart from the awesome carpaccio of zebra in our favourite restaurant, the Brauhaus) is the dunes – massive, mountainous acres of unspoilt sand that ring the town and shelve steeply down towards the sea. Dave was determined to fly over them by microlight and persuaded me that it was something I had to do too. The idea was certainly appealing; the reality was that the only time Dave had tried to take me flying before, the struggle between gravity and two big lads in a go-cart with wings had not gone our way. In fact, we'd ended up in a hedge at the end of the runway. But this time, equipped with a bigger engine, we soared into the air like…well, like two big lads in a go-cart. But it was the most incredible, unforgettable experience, and thankfully the clean pair of trousers I'd stuffed in my pannier weren't required.

> 'Finding two wetsuits for blokes our size wasn't easy, but Paul did his best. Unfortunately, his best had me in a turquoise condom that would have been tight on Kate Moss, while Dave was levered into some kind of Russian survival suit.'

The local crayfish in Swakopmund are superb, so we enlisted Paul's help to catch some. Finding two wetsuits for blokes our size wasn't easy, but Paul did his best. Unfortunately, his best had me in a turquoise condom that would have been tight on Kate Moss, while Dave was levered into some kind of Russian survival suit that made him look like a bouncy castle from a kids' playground in Murmansk. 'Hmm...' said Stroudie, surveying us; 'in the darker reaches of the Internet there are weird sites dedicated to this sort of thing.' I didn't ask him how he knew this; breathing was difficult enough without trying to talk as well. We lolloped into the sea in search of our prey, and believe me, you haven't lived till you've been knocked off your feet for the fifth time by an Atlantic roller while all around you crayfish wipe tears of laughter from their beady little eyes with their claws.

Our last night in Swakopmund was a frantic round of packing, checking, stowing and loading. We'd been using a beach house as a base, and Dave had made about twenty trips between bedroom and bike through the sliding patio doors. At which point, Stroudie wandered through the living-room and closed them. The noise from Dave's twenty-first trip, when the Myers nose unexpectedly hit 10mm of reinforced glass at some speed, had nearby residents grabbing grandfather's Luger from its display case. 'God, I'm so sorry!' said the director; 'I only shut them because of the smell from the beach.' 'I can't smell owt,' said Dave, ice-pack on a nose that had been a different shape and size only a moment before. It is of course cruel to laugh when your mate's injured – but we howled anyway.

We rolled out of Swakopmund the next morning and headed north, running on the salt road parallel to the ocean. First port of call was the seal colony at Cape Cross: around 80,000 seals barking, fighting and...smelling. While thousands of big brown eyes look up at you sweetly, the stench nearly knocks you off your feet. 'It's like Glastonbury for seals,' remarked Dave. We pitched camp the first night at Messum Crater, an awesome place. As you head inland from the ocean, you say goodbye to roads for the next thousand kilometres. In their place, the track turns greyer and darker as you enter an extraordinary volcanic world. Nothing lives here, nothing grows here – apart from the occasional myrrh bush. It really did feel like being on Mars; and the most unnerving thing was the silence. When the fire had burnt down and the crew had turned in, all that was left was...nothing. However hard you strained your ears, there was no tree to rustle, no bird to chirp, no distant motorway traffic, no planes overhead. Paul reckons, if you listen very hard in Messum Crater, you can hear the Earth turn.

Beyond Messum was the Namibia we'd read and dreamt about. The dust roads rolled on and on through the bush, past massive granite mountains and through treacherously soft river beds. We got used to seeing springbok everywhere, along with the gnarly horns of the oryx and the mad bustle of ostriches at full speed. And best of all, there was a wonderful sense of emptiness, of being in a place where you could ride all day and maybe pass one other vehicle.

DAVE: And all the while, it was getting hotter. We reached the extraordinary Giribes Plain, north of Sesfontein, which is covered in hundreds of fairy circles. The botanists have been trying to work out for decades why the desert grass will not grow in these patches; we were just concerned about getting a decent fire going for our earth-roasted lamb. So as the thermometer climbed to nearly 45°C, the middle of the day was spent shovelling hot coals into a hole in the ground. Not one of our best ideas, in retrospect, although the lamb tasted really good.

While we were preparing the meal, Paul's mate Gerry was dispatched to scout for wildlife. To call Paul or Gerry an animal tracker is like saying Delia can cook a bit – it's not quite the whole story. Gerry turned up at camp an hour later with news. 'Nice herd of elephant going down the river bed. Six of them – Big Toe's there, two cows and three juveniles, one quite young. They're moving slowly, eating well – we'll meet them just past the bluff at about 2 p.m.' We were already impressed. 'Blimey. How close were you when you saw them?' 'Aw,' grinned Gerry, 'haven't seen them yet.' And at 2 p.m., just past the bluff, we did meet them. Now that's tracking.

Namibia's desert elephants are rare creatures; there's probably only a few hundred of them left in the wild. So to find yourself in the same river bed as a small herd was an unforgettable experience. We stood by the Land Rover as they slowly made their way past us, browsing the thick leaves on the opposite bank. Then Big Toe, the bull, began to focus on us. There was a tiny movement of the head, a setting of the shoulders, and then Gerry's calm instruction: 'Into the vehicle. He's charging.' You've never seen two big blokes try to get into the same car seat so quickly. In fact, Big Toe was merely proving a point: we were on his turf, and the right thing to do was to show submission and withdraw. Which we did, quite quickly.

Besides, the lamb was nearly done. After which we had the traditional Namibian spitting-the-springbok-dropping competition to look forward to. 'We can use raisins or summat, can't we, Stroudie?' 'Reality is all, dear boys, reality is all,' he smiled, helping himself to another glass of Colombard. Wait till he finds out what we've put in his sleeping bag.

THE SPRINGBOKDROL VERSPOEGKOMPETIESIE (or, as we say, The Springbok-drool Far-spitti Competissi)

This is one of Namibia's national recreations. The cup finals are held annually in Usakos and Karibib, where gladiators of the sport gather to do battle.

Well, it's not quite the Olympics or cup-final day, but it does have a certain charm. A bunch of men get together and the game goes something like this: you take a bowl of springbok droppings – yes, a bowl of little turds – soak them in plum schnapps to take away the gamey flavour, then you see how far you can spit the little jobbies. It's great fun, costs very little and keeps you amused for hours. And it's a sport you can play anywhere, as we found out in the fairy circles of Giribes. One night, Si set out the white helmet as a target (um, my helmet – because it would show up better in the setting sun, he said), I gathered the droppings – there are thousands once you start to look; a herd of springbok roaming free does produce a lot of poo – and then I pickled some prime ammo in the fruity liquor. Then we chose our weapons and let rip. Indeed, a springbok turd is the perfect shape and size for a good hockle. Pow, ping, splat . . . droppings bounced off my helmet. It really is an addictive hobby. But please can we use Si's helmet next time?

In fact, Dave and I became real poo connoisseurs in Namibia. When examining droppings of the inhabitants of the savannah, the one striking fact is how every drop of moisture is extracted from the diet to get the animals through the dry season. And there are other fascinating details: hyena poo, for instance, is white because of the amount of bone, and therefore calcium, in its diet. And when you break the dry husk of the wonderful rhino's droppings, the smell of cologne hits you right in the mush. What is responsible for this sophisticated odour, I hear you ask. Well, it's the fantastic aroma of the ancient myrrh bush (yes, the Three Kings' myrrh), which grows freely in the desert and is a staple of the rhino's diet. Honestly, if you could bottle it you'd wear it. And the best poo for keeping mosquitoes away is elephant dung. Light it and a not unpleasant smoke and aroma is emitted, a bit like a joss stick on steroids. It really does keep the little blighters at bay. Dave took great pleasure in juggling with the bits we didn't light. It was messy but the exercise did him good.

DAVE: Our quest throughout the long trip north had been to try to make contact with the Himba, a nomadic tribe who still hold fast to their traditional way of life. To finally meet up with them was a real privilege; we were guided around their village and shown how they prepare the red paste with which the women adorn their bodies. Their huts were not really designed for the likes of us, and at one point I had a vision of Kingy stuck in the tiny entrance like Pooh in Rabbit's burrow. But it was a unique glimpse into another culture, and we wouldn't have missed it for the world.

SI: Cooking for the Himba was the perfect way to end our trip. We could see them approaching, just tiny figures in the heat haze of the savannah, but we had no idea how the meal would be received. In fact we needn't have worried; it turned out to be one of the most enjoyable parties you could imagine. Dave's bobotie was a triumph, the fruit kebabs disappeared within seconds, and the sun began to set to the sound of much, much laughter.

There's always a note of regret when a trip comes to an end, but round the campfire that night was particularly poignant. We'd been lucky enough to ride through a real wilderness, and to meet some extraordinary people. We'd eaten some great game, succulent seafood, and learned how to cook in a hole in the ground. But crucially, Dave had fallen off more times than I had. Perfect.

'Africa always takes something from you but the gifts she bestows will be far in excess of what she takes and the memory of her beauty and serenity will last a lifetime.'

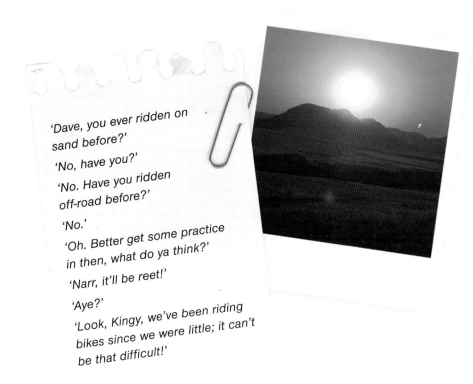

'Dave, you ever ridden on sand before?'

'No, have you?'

'No. Have you ridden off-road before?'

'No.'

'Oh. Better get some practice in then, what do ya think?'

'Narr, it'll be reet!'

'Aye?'

'Look, Kingy, we've been riding bikes since we were little; it can't be that difficult!'

BIKE BITS

An hour had passed and we were making steady progress. The first half hour had been given to zoning out in complete concentration; the rest of the time was spent giggling and shouting 'Whoopee!' in that irritating American way. We stopped for our first drink of water, got off the bikes ... and stood on the sharpest surface we had ever encountered. Small stones and rocks, filed over millennia to a razor's edge by the heat and wind, lay in wait for us and our tyres under a layer of red dust. 'Shit! We forgot to lower the tyre pressures and to switch off the ABS!' A mistake we did not repeat. If we had piled it in that environment we would have been sushi, and we both realised we needed to turn the concentration levels up to 11.

The film crew and our tracker caught up and briefed us on the next stage of the route (we always tried hard to lose them, much to the annoyance of our director and cameraman). 'It goes through a very environmentally sensitive area, lads, so it is imperative that you navigate within the boundaries of the track – oh, and you'll have to ride through a river bed.' 'OK,' we replied. 'Should we crack on then?'

And it came to pass that river beds were our nemesis. In Namibia (and most of Africa), river beds are giant sandpits of varying depths and grades of sand. Particularly nasty are the partially covered rocks that've been thrown in just for fun. The only way to get you and the bike through safely is to ride fast and get the bike on a plane, much the same as a speed-boat gets through water. Theoretically, this keeps the front wheel up and the rear wheel tractoring through the soft stuff. If you don't do it that way, you fall off, simple as that.

The problem with this technique is that every basic instinct is screaming 'Slow down, you idiot,' and of course you do and, guess what, you fall off. And sand is a very unforgiving mistress: I can only liken it to being hit square in the chest by a three-tonne bag of flour. We fell off with such alarming regularity it was like playing a warped game of bingo in which the gods shouted HOUSE! on your behalf, just for a laugh. We did eventually wise up and develop a kind of survival routine that went like this: front end breaks away, you fall off. Initial impact, you and bike = large mushroom cloud. Roll out of cloud to await that moment of a) is the bike OK? b) has Dave hit the same trap? c) are my arms and legs still attached to my torso as God intended? If so, get help to pick bike up and continue. Now, this really does mess with your head, but we had no alternative but to bash on.

We had totally underestimated how difficult off-road riding is, particularly on sand. In addition we had not given the terrain the respect it deserved; looking out of the window of a Land Rover and riding a bike through a tough wilderness are two totally different disciplines. This was never so apparent as when the crew would catch up and enthuse, 'Guys, did you see that giraffe?' or 'the fantastic light on that mountain?' We would look at them, faces like bags of hammers, and say: 'Do you lot think this is easy? All we've seen is the road and the middle distance so that we can live long enough to finish making the programme!'

We arrived at Messum Crater three hours later than planned. Dusk was descending, and indeed Africa had taken something from us – chunks from our shins (on those bloody BMW R1200GS pots), twisted knees, strained backs and mental exhaustion. But it was all worth it. We had never been part of such beauty, scale and serenity as we were in that landscape on our first night in the wilderness. That night was to set the tone for the rest of our adventure and subsequent love affair with Namibia.

'We arrived at Messum Crater three hours later than planned. Dusk was descending, and indeed Africa had taken something from us – chunks from our shins, twisted knees, strained backs and mental exhaustion.'

Should you be fortunate enough to go biking in Namibia there are a few words of advice we would give. First, the wildlife is very important, not only to the Namibian infrastructure but also to the planet we all share. A delicate balance must be maintained between tourism and the wonder of the flora, fauna and wildlife. Secondly, the environment is unforgiving – if you don't have enough water or fuel, or if you get lost, you will be lucky to get out alive. The best way to keep everyone safe, in our view, is to hire a Namibian guide. It will undoubtedly increase the cost of your trip but you will live to ride another day and it will make your stay and memories truly epic. Oh, and they drive on the left, which makes life easier for us Brits and a few others. Prior to leaving home, an old mate of eighty-two years (and still firing on all four cylinders) said to me, 'Africa always takes something from you but the gifts she bestows will be far in excess of what she takes and the memory of her beauty and serenity will last a lifetime.' I must be honest, I didn't fully appreciate his words until we were well on the road. We'd known the route we wanted to take, we had asked local advice, taken the warnings seriously and questioned our skill levels. But nothing could have prepared us for the interior of Namibia.

Dave and I left the relative security of Swakopmund's tarmac and salt roads on a misty Sunday morning, just after dawn. A word of warning about salt roads: if they get wet, which is often the case in Swakopmund due to the mist belt on the coast, they become slippy. And I don't mean proceed-with-caution slippy, I mean road-rash-exfoliation slippy.

It was our intention to ride to Messum Crater – an ancient and surreal landscape that looks like a Roger Dean album cover – and make camp. It was hot as we turned off the highway, as directed. A large pile of rocks marked the barely visible track leading towards a landscape the like of which we had never seen, and, beyond that, the foothills of the great Mount Brandburg. We remembered the advice of our guides: if you're ahead of us, be sure you know your route because if you get lost you die. It really is as simple as that. 'Are you shitting yourself, mate?' I asked Dave. 'Bloody right. Are you?' 'Hell, yes.' 'Let's away then.' That's the good thing about riding with your best mate; it never takes long to sort out the rules of engagement.

MICROLIGHT-FLYING;
or Three-dimensional Biking

DAVE: I first learnt to fly microlights about five years ago. I went to the motorcycle show in Manchester and saw her: bright yellow, with a disproportionately large engine – like a motorbike with a 30-foot wingspan. I got talking, and in true hairy-biker style, got an overdraft and presented myself at the airfield. This was the beginning of a love-hate-and-shit-yourself two years to get my licence. Finally, on a grey February day, I made my first solo flight. There is nothing more liberating and more terrifying.

Now, in Africa three years later, with a good hundred flying hours under my belt, all my dreams were to come true: flying around Africa with my best mate. As ever, it wasn't that easy...First I had to get an African flying licence, an African radio licence, mega-insurance and a bit of African flying. So three weeks prior to filming, Si and I flew to Namibia to begin our prep. The first five days were to be spent sorting out the flying, so we drove to Omeruru to meet Boris, who was going to test me. We arrived that evening to find that the airfield was about a thousand metres of dirt – I mean rough, dusty dirt, and no windsock or any of the normal bits and pieces.

Boris said that the best plan was to take off at first light and fly into the sunrise, so the next morning I drove to the airfield and we waited for dawn. The chief mechanic, Snake-eye (so called because he lost his right eye to a cobra), wheeled the aircraft from the hangar. The first whiff of trouble came when he used a cut-down water bottle as a funnel to refuel the plane. Now, at home we are fastidious: no dust, and all the fuel is filtered. Muck in the carbs is the easiest way to have engine failure. Lined up on the runway, I started the preflight checks. Some of the instruments seemed to be missing, but, reassured by Boris that all was well, I throttled down the runway and took off. It was like flying a brick, but, miraculously, one circuit later I landed perfectly. Boris jumped out, said I'd passed, that I could help myself to the plane, and that the garage was down the road if I wanted more fuel. And that was it – bye!

Our Toyota appeared and Kingy emerged. 'How's it going, mate?' 'Passed,' I replied. 'Put your helmet on, we're going for a ride.' It was Si's first flight (we never got further than the hedge the only time we tried back home). We backtracked along the runway, made preflight checks on instruments that didn't exist, and, on full throttle, took off.

It was one of the best moments of our lives. We flew over the bush towards the mountains, navigating as well as we could with just a compass and no map. We saw zebra and giraffe and swooped low over the dried-up river bed as the animals grazed, taking care not to disturb them. Kingy could say little except 'Eeh, man! Ooh, Dave, dude, why-egh!' It was like having Lindisfarne in the back seat.

That night, Boris came round. Could we do him a favour? Now, as well as running the local gun and ammo shop and being a part-time pilot, he was also a local politician. He had a delegation of the Swedish government staying in Omeruru, and had promised them flights at dawn over the savannah. As we were limited for time, would I share the flying with him? I explained that as I had perhaps two hours' flying in Africa and was a relatively new pilot it would not be a good idea. His curling lip gave me the answer, so dawn the next day found Kingy, myself and twelve members of the Swedish government standing by the hangar.

Boris arrived and wheeled an even more knackered aircraft out. I strapped in a very serious Swede and took off. 'Hi,' I said, 'what's your name?' A whimper came back: 'Chris.' 'And what do you do, Chris?' 'I'm Minister for Rural Development. How long have you been a bush pilot?' 'Ooh, ages,' I said. 'Do you think we will see much wildlife?' he asked. 'Should do,' I replied, whilst all the time thinking: We will be bloody lucky not to get lost and to get back in one piece. But right on cue, a family of giraffe appeared below us. And that was it: from then on I was the mutt's nuts. Six flights later I taxied back to the hangar with a new career ... to find Kingy dispensing coffee, blagging a free holiday and trying to score a cheap Volvo.

It was worth all the hassle for the experience of a lifetime. If you like bikes, you will love microlights. It is true flying, and a good way for the ordinary person to take to the skies. Have a go.

FOOD BITS

Namibia is really old and it feels old; in fact when mankind first got off all fours and developed lumbago it was probably in Namibia. About four million years ago the earliest upright walking humanoids kicked off on the savannahs of southern Africa. Then about two and a half million years later they started using tools, so now they could hunt for food instead of just scavenging. And the prevalence of game on the savannah meant it was a prehistoric superstore waiting to happen. On one archaeological site in the Namibian desert there is proof that people were capturing and butchering elephants at this time.

Thus, dear reader, we make the conclusion that this is a real old-food culture: great game, chuck in some fire, and we have the basis of a gastronomy. For a couple of million years nothing changed; the indigenous people – whose descendants today make up the San, Khoisan, Herero, Himba, Damara and Owambo peoples – enjoyed relative peace and an endless barbecue. They had adapted to the harsh terrain, could farm, mine minerals and produce textiles. There were a few outsiders: in the mid-sixteenth century the good old Portuguese arrived in the shape of Captain Diego Cao, who sailed as far as Cape Cross looking for a route to the Indies. Ten years later his countryman Bartolomeu Dias came to what is now Luderitz, en route to the Cape of Good Hope.

The first real colonials were the Brits, who came looking for guano (bird poo), a nitrate from which you can make high explosives. When you have an empire to run guano is hot stuff…and smelly too! Then, in the nineteenth century, Adolf Luderitz petitioned Bismarck to place the region under German 'protection'. They came, stole all the sun beds, the Brits left, and Namibia became a German protectorate. After the First World War, it came under the mandate of South Africa, and finally, after a long guerrilla war between SWAPO and South Africa, Namibia became independent in 1990. But parts of it are still so German, giving the country a very eccentric, almost other-worldly feel, almost as if Dr Livingstone and the cradle of humanity had been crossed with a Düsseldorf suburb.

We arrived in Swakopmund just as dusk was falling. As we rode down Richthofen Street on to Bismarck Street looking for the hotel Schweizerhaus, we felt that oddness; all is ordered and clinical, rather like driving into a retirement town for the SS. Then you turn a corner and the desert of your dreams appears: rolling sand dunes over a hundred metres high that stretch from the edge of town for hundreds of kilometres. It's all very strange.

Underneath the Schweizerhaus is the Café Anton, a full-blown Salzburg coffee house serving good coffee, strudel and their famous Black Forest gâteau. There isn't a sniff of a leopard print here; instead there's a mural of the Rhine on the wall, an imperial eagle above the door and oom-pah music in the background. Feeling hungry, we ate at the excellent Swakopmund Brauhaus, on Kaiser Wilhelm Street. It is a German beerhouse and serves really, really traditional German food – pork knuckle and sauerkraut, spaetzles and wienersnitzel – but look closer and they also serve zebra carpaccio, oryx and springbok. By the way, raw zebra with a dressing of olive oil and a misting of Parmesan is one of the tastiest and best meats I have ever had.

Now, the beer: the main employer in the town is the long-established Hansa Brewery. The local brew, Tafel, is produced to the old German purity laws of the Reinheitsgebot. It is nectar, one of the best beers in the world: come in from the desert, look at a foaming pint of Tafel with condensation on the glass, and it's *Ice Cold in Alex* and Gollum's first glimpse of the Ring rolled into one. Then go to the Tug, a seafood restaurant built in an old boat. Have more Tafel and a dozen Walvis Bay oysters, the biggest you have ever seen, then a simple grilled Atlantic sole washed down with a crisp sauvignon blanc, and life is not so rough.

It wasn't, however, like this for the Boer settlers. For them, life was rougher than a rhino with eczema. One of their staples was biltong, dried meat that weighed a third of raw meat, so was easier to carry and lasted for months. There is still a whole biltong culture. It can be made from beef, ostrich, springbok, oryx, or any other meat you can find. Each has a different character, and nowadays it is often spiced with chillies, herbs and piri-piri (the chilli bites are awesome with a cool pint of Tafel). They also make dried sausage called dryworst, which is very tasty, and you can buy biltong powder, which can be stirred into cream cheese and put in sandwiches, or mixed with sour cream for dips. Si's favourite was beesbiltong, 50 per cent beef and 50 per cent dried balls of fat. Well, he is young, fit and healthy – but not for long if he keeps scoffing that.

In Peter's Antiques we learnt more about the Boers' food. Peter, an old-school German, sells fine African antiquities and German military memorabilia, and has written a cookbook of traditional German and Boer recipes. Top of his pops is puff adder (first catch the puff, a seriously venomous snake). He also has recipes for elephant heart that would feed a few (and you can make umbrella stands with the left-over legs!) and more traditional roasts like leg of zebra, which is very tasty. He also has a chilling sign in his shop: 'Shoplifters Take Note: Stock Protected by Voodoo'. *Auf wiedersehen*, pet!

Another snack that is often washed down with Tafel is mopane worms. These are an Owambo delicacy, and are from hell. They are basically sun-dried caterpillars, collected from the mopani tree and laid out on roofs. First you notice the sandy crunch; this is the

hundreds of tiny legs. Then the taste of rotting beef hits your palette. Then you bite into the middle and the taste of mouldering trainers hits the cortex of your brain...EEOW. After subduing the gagging reflex we got our worms down, at which point our cameraman, in his droll Scottish way, said 'I didn't quite get that, would you mind eating some more?' Seriously, though, they are a good source of protein and have often supported people for long periods – though I think personally I would have thrown in the towel.

Game of all sorts is readily available in Namibia. It's cheaper than beef and as some of the farms are about the size of an English county, the stuff is as free range as you can get. They are shot as required, so the meat is fresh, and they hang the meat properly – no EU nonsense. There is a freedom in Namibia: if you need something done you do it; if you need food you get it. Take the local crayfish. They are the size of lobsters, but a permit costs about 15p per day, and entitles you to take six. That's good value. Well, you do have to catch them first. 'Oh, it's simple guys,' said our friend Paul. 'We get a wetsuit, snorkel and get them off the seabed.' Well it was simple for Paul. I was in that Second World War Russian immersion suit and was more buoyant than Jordan's bust. We cooked the crayfish we caught in our rock-salt tandoori, using salt we gathered from the salt pans outside Swakopmund, and ate them with asparagus rice. Yum.

As well as the excellent raw ingredients, the other important influence on Namibian cuisine arrived in the 1600s, when the Dutch East India Company stopped at the Cape en route to Java. Spice farms were planted and thousands of Malay slaves from Java were brought over to work the plantations. They brought with them their unique spicy cooking, and the resulting Cape Malay cuisine has been respected and enjoyed for over two hundred years. Then the country came under South African control in the early twentieth century, and the alchemy of the two traditions is pretty straightforward: a sweet and sour fusion of meat, fruit, curry and spices.

In 1946, Dr Christian Leipoldt, a great Cape Town surgeon, chef and wine connoisseur, wrote *Leipoldt's Cape Cookery*. In it he writes: 'I had an interest in cookery dating back to the 1880s when, just a small boy, under the guidance of a spotless, if obese, expert Cape Coloured woman, I greedily devoured her culinary magic and expertise in the preparation of Malay cookery. The Ayah's art was the result of many years of instruction and experience in the traditional methods of Malay cookery, whose outstanding characteristics are the free, almost heroic use of spices and aromatic flavourings, the prolonged, steady, but slow application of heat to all meat dishes and the skilful blending of many diverse constituents into a combination that still holds the essential goodness of each.' This seems to sum up Namibian cooking: it is soul food with roots.

MAGIC STARTERS

Well, to start on the fruit and meat vibe, we came up with a couple of belters. Don't be put off by the game meat; these snacks are just as good with pork and lamb.

SPRINGBOK (OR PORK)
With Himbas on Horseback

Serves 4 as a starter

200g loin of springbok or pork, cubed
10 slices streaky bacon
10 dates, stoned

Take the springbok or pork, cube and season. Wrap each date in a stretched-out piece of the bacon – the thinner it is the crispier it will be. Thread on to skewers alternate pieces of meat and bacon-wrapped date. Cook on the barbie, or under a medium grill, for 20 minutes, turning occasionally. The combination is ace.

KUDU (OR LAMB), PINEAPPLE AND GREEN-PEPPER KEBABS

These three flavours work really well together: the spicy meat with the juicy, fruity pineapple with the sharpness of the green pepper.

Serves 4 as a starter

for the rub	1 tspn rock salt
2 tspns ground cumin	250g kudu or lamb fillet, cubed
½ tspn crushed black pepper	250g pineapple (a 454g tin, drained)
½ tspn chilli flakes	1 green pepper, cut into 2cm squares
¼ tspn cayenne pepper	olive oil

Mix the spices and salt, and then add the cubed meat. Leave for half an hour if possible, then thread the meat, pineapple and pepper on to the skewers. Drizzle with a little olive oil before cooking for about 5 minutes on each side, turning regularly. If you're inside, allow plenty of ventilation as the rub is quite pungent.

THE BIG-GAME BARBIE

CROCODILE (OR PORK)
With Cashew-nut Satay

Crocodile is readily available in Africa; harder to find in Bognor obviously, but this dish is just as good with pork, chicken, beef or prawns.

Serves 4 as a snack

250g crocodile or pork fillet
juice of 1 lemon
3 tbs olive oil
2 cloves garlic, crushed
2 tbs soy sauce

for the satay sauce
4 tbs crunchy peanut butter
100g cashew nuts, crushed

juice of 1 lime
½ tin of coconut milk
chilli to taste
1 tbs soy sauce
sugar to taste
a splash of pineapple juice

Cut the meat into strips about 1cm wide, then into 2cm chunks. Season well. Mix the other ingredients together and marinate the meat for a good half hour.

Whizz the peanut butter, cashews and lime juice together in a blender, then stir in the coconut milk, soy sauce and pineapple juice. Simmer over a gentle heat for 5 minutes, adding more pineapple juice to get the consistency you like.

Thread the crocodile on to the skewers and place on the barbecue or griddle. Cook for 4 minutes on each side, basting throughout. Be careful not to overcook them. Serve with the hot sauce.

ORYX (OR VENISON) Stuffed With Blue Cheese and Cranberries

This is a sweet and sour sensation – crispy on the outside, juicy in the middle and it's more tender than Elvis Presley when he is getting all romantic.

Serves 8

1kg oryx fillet (or venison), cut into thin steaks
olive oil
200g blue cheese
½ jar of cranberry sauce

If the meat is a bit tough, put the steaks between two pieces of clingfilm and beat until really thin; this makes the meat tender and gives the texture that you want. Oil the steaks and season, although don't add too much salt – there is a lot already in the blue cheese. Mash the cheese and the cranberry sauce until smooth, then spread a thorough layer on to each steak and roll them up like swiss rolls. Secure the ends with cocktail sticks and cook on the fire for about 10 minutes. The meat will be well cooked on the outside and very rare in the middle – perfect.

OSTRICH (OR DUCK) AND PEAR TERIYAKI

Of all the game meats, ostrich is the most easy to get hold of as it is available in some butchers' and even supermarkets. It has a lovely flavour and is very low in cholesterol. Go on, give it a go.

Serves 5

1kg ostrich fillet (or duck breast)
2 firm pears, cut into 1cm cubes
bunch of spring onions, trimmed, halved
  lengthways and cut into 2cm pieces

for the teriyaki sauce
115ml light soy sauce
30ml mirin rice wine or sake
½ tspn sugar

Cut the ostrich into very thin strips – think carpaccio. Take a chunk of pear and a strip of spring onion and wrap the sheet of ostrich around them. Thread on to a skewer and repeat. When you have a heap of kebabs, marinate in the teriyaki sauce for 1 hour while you bury your head in the sand. Cook for about 2 minutes each side over a hot fire or under the grill.

PROPER BURGERS

We used zebra meat for this recipe and it was delicious. I know what you're thinking though: zebra meat is not readily available in the UK unless you live near a zoo. However, you can use minced beef, lamb or pork instead, so no excuse for not giving it a try. The point of the recipe is to involve the kids in the preparation of food they'll want to eat – no waste then, you see, and some time spent with the gang getting a bit messy.

Makes 4 large burgers

455g mince

4 shallots, chopped fine

1 tbs fresh thyme if you're using beef
(1 tbs mint for lamb or ½ tbs sage for pork)

1 clove garlic (or more to taste),
finely chopped

freshly ground black pepper

3 good pinches of salt

a dash of tabasco, or chopped
chillies to taste

olive oil

Put all the ingredients into a big bowl. Wash your hands and go for it: squish thoroughly so all the ingredients are mixed evenly through the meat. Don't be reluctant to season – you'll get it right! Wait for a bit (as long as you can – maybe half an hour) to let the flavours get into the meat, then form into burgers, brush with olive oil and put on the barbecue or in the frying pan until brown and crispy on the outside.

GEM SQUASH
Filled With Mozzarella and Celery Leaves

Use celery leaves in this simple dish as they are packed with flavour and are great in soups too. Why do we usually throw them away?

Serves 8

1 gem squash per person
olive oil
mozzarella, preferably buffalo
celery leaves, finely chopped

Split the squash into two and de-seed. Pour a teaspoon of olive oil into each cavity and season. Place a cube of mozzarella about the size of a matchbox in the holes and top with a tablespoon of finely chopped celery leaves. Wrap in foil and throw into the fire or moderate oven for about 20 minutes. Fabulous.

SWAKOPMUND ASPARAGUS AND BUTTER RICE

They love to serve vegetable rice with fish all over Africa, and it works well as a great side dish. A drizzle from the dips on page 71 is also fab on the rice, as is a hunk of the crayfish.

Serves 2

2 cups of rice
6 cups of salted water
1 bunch asparagus, cut into 1cm pieces
big knob of unsalted butter

Cook the rice using the absorption method: for every measure of rice, add three measures of cold water to a saucepan and bring to the boil. Simmer gently until the water has all been absorbed or read individual packets for instructions as all types and brands of rice seem to be different. About 5 minutes before the rice is done, throw in the asparagus. When all is ready, add the butter.

SALT-BAKED CRAYFISH
With Three Dips

This is a wonderful way of cooking crayfish, lobster or langoustine, with whole spices buried in the hot salt. The heat releases the scents and flavours of the spices and they delicately perfume the shellfish.

Serves 2

12 large crayfish (or crevettes)
2kg rough rock salt
20 star anise

a small handful of coriander seeds
a small handful of whole peppercorns
2 lemons, halved

Wipe a large, deep, cast-iron pan clean with a slice of lemon then pour in the rock salt to a depth of at least 5cm; bury the star anise, coriander seeds and peppercorns randomly and put on the fire or in an oven at 180°C. When hot, the effect is a bit like a tandoori oven and the star anise starts to fume. Bury the crayfish and sit the lemons (skin-side down) on top. Cover with a tent of foil that fits tightly around the pan but allows for the perfumed air to circulate and bake for 10–15 minutes depending on the size of your catch.

If you're feeling flush and have splashed out on lobster tails or big crays, then split them length ways, remove the alimentary canal (the black stringy bit that runs down the length of the tail) and stack, shell-side down, on top of the salt. Cover and bake as above for 10-15 minutes depending on the size and the number of tails.

Garlic butter

Melt 125g butter, being careful not to burn it. Add 1 teaspoon crushed black peppercorns and 4 or 5 cloves of garlic that have been lightly bruised. Take off the heat and leave to infuse.

Lemon butter

Melt 125g butter. Add the zest of 1 lemon and about 1 tablespoon of lemon juice. You could also add a sprig of lemon thyme if you have it. Leave to infuse. If this is too sour, balance with a bit of sugar.

Soy sauce with ginger

This is a antidote to the heavy buttery sauces. Take 200ml soy sauce, add 1 chopped chilli and 1 teaspoon of grated ginger.

Then, when the crayfish are cooked, simply peel the tails and dip into the sauces. This is about as good as food gets.

MAGIC LAMB Cooked With Biblical Berries in an African Fairy Circle on the Flames of the Tree of Life

We cooked this in the fairy circles at Gerebes on the Namibian savannah using a traditional Himba cooking method. It's not as daft as it sounds: the weight of the soil acts as a pressure cooker giving you the tenderest roast meat imaginable. You can use the oven if you live in a flat; otherwise go and dig up your lawn. It will be unforgettable.

Serves 6–8

2½ kg leg of lamb
olive oil
salt and pepper
garlic

rosemary
3 or 4 anchovy fillets
handful of lion-bush berries
(or some green peppercorns and/or pomegranate seeds)

First dig a rectangular hole about 2 feet deep. Then light a big bonfire with wood from the Tree of Life, the omumboronbonga tree, known locally as leadwood or ironwood (or any old dry wood will do). Leave to burn down to white coals.

Meanwhile, give the lamb a good rub with the olive oil, season well, stab holes all over the meat and in them plant bits of garlic, rosemary and the odd anchovy. Liberally sprinkle with the lion-bush berries (green peppercorns and/or pomegranate seeds). Wrap the joint in 7 layers of foil, some one way and some the other. The meat must be sealed and dust-proof. Then fill the bottom of your pit with about 4cm of hot coals. Lay the lamb gently onto this, then cover the sides and top with the remainder of the coals. Bury with dry sand or soil to ground level. The lamb will need to be left for about 3 hours to cook. Something special happens with this way of cooking.

If you're closer to Sidcup than Swakopmund, you can cook your lamb in an oven at 170°C for about 2½ hours, removing the foil for the last 20 minutes.

In a second pit do your veggies in a similar way, but for about half an hour (or for about 45 minutes in the same oven as the lamb). We used butternut and gem squash, sweet potatoes, mixed peppers, whole heads of garlic and half onions, dressed with olive oil, rosemary, salt and pepper. Result: feast!

THE GRAND FINALE

BOBOTIE

The great bobotie is a kind of fruity, herby meatloaf with a curried custard topping – sounds awful but tastes great! Most southern Africans have their own recipe; ours is a classic with a heap of local advice thrown in.

Serves about 20

for the meatloaf

3kg best beef mince; better still, get good rump steak and mince it yourself
250g blanched almonds (coarsely chopped)
about 25 peppercorns, crushed
thumb-size piece fresh ginger, grated
2 hot chillies, de-seeded and finely chopped
a few sprigs marjoram
about 20 coriander seeds, crushed
4 cloves garlic, peeled and crushed
1 small onion, peeled and finely chopped
grated zest of 1 lemon
handful sultanas
285ml good red wine
½ tspn tamarind or 1 tbs lemon juice

125g unsalted butter, melted
250ml double cream
salt and pepper
8 bay leaves
cumin seeds

for the custard topping

565ml milk
10 eggs
2 tbs old-fashioned curry powder
1 tspn baking powder
salt

to serve

a good grating of nutmeg

In a large bowl, put all the ingredients up to and including the sultanas and get stuck in with your bare hands so that they are all thoroughly mixed together. Butter the largest caserole dish you can find, cover the bottom with cumin seeds, then transfer the mixture. In a measuring jug, put the red wine, tamarind, melted butter, double cream, salt and pepper. Pour over the mince and fork through to allow it to permeate the meat. Plant the bay leaves like seedlings in the top then cover and bake until cooked through and risen: about 90 minutes at 180°C.

Whisk the custard ingredients together, pour over the loaves and bake for 20 minutes or until set and a golden-brown. You can finish it off with a blowtorch if it looks a bit anaemic. Finish with a flourish of grated nutmeg. Great bonfire-night grub.

PAUL AND GERRY'S NAMIBIAN PAP
With Biltong Powder

Pap (cornmeal) is a staple in Africa and the preparation of it is a varied art form: there are as many ways to prepare it as there are people eating it, and believe us that is an awful lot. This recipe was given to us by our guides and good mates, Paul and Gerry, who are experts in the preparation of large-scale portions of pap over an open fire in the wonderful wilderness of Namibia. Gerry is so dedicated to protecting the wildlife from poachers that he hasn't slept in a bed for the past fifteen years; so you can imagine how much he cooks the stuff. We could not have wished for two better teachers of this noble and ancient art.

Serves about 6

1 litre water
125g butter
good pinch of salt
325–350g pap (cornmeal)

olive oil
biltong powder (or slivers of salami
  or dry-cured ham)

In a large pan, put your water, butter and salt. Bring the water to just below the boil. Then, stirring all the time with a wooden spoon, sprinkle the pap onto the surface of the water a little at a time – be patient, it takes a while but it's worth it. You should get to the point that the pap starts to form bubbles on the surface, kind of like a thick semolina consistency. (Be careful: it's bloody hot at this stage.) Keep stirring and add more butter and salt, some pepper and your biltong powder, salami or ham.

Eventually you will find it very hard to stir. Now, this is the good bit: at the point when stirring becomes impossible, the pap will become separated from the side of the pan. Push the wooden spoon in between the pan and the pap, work your way around the pan and all the pap should come away. Pour olive oil around the perimeter of the pan to form a layer between it and the pap. You will need to repeat this process at least three times.

It is hard to describe how to achieve the perfect pap. You will eventually be able to do it by sight and feel. Please persevere: it really is good craic on an open fire, and a change to bread at a barbecue.

FRUIT KEBABS
With a Chocolate, Orange and Rum Sauce

You can use whatever fruit you fancy for these – pineapple, pear, dates, apple, banana – but think of fruit that will caramelise.

Serves 6–8

for the kebabs
good selection of fruit, cubed as necessary
sesame seeds
Muscavado sugar or honey

for the sauce
200g good plain chocolate
  (70% cocoa solids)
juice of 1 orange
2 tbs dark rum
285ml double cream
100g caster sugar

Thread the kebabs up and sprinkle with the sesame seeds and the sugar (honey could also be used). Cook on the fire or grill for about 3 minutes, until the sugar has caramelised and the fruit is scorched.

In a bain-marie (a bowl lodged above a pan of boiling water), melt the chocolate, whisk in the cream and add the rum and orange juice. Watch the sauce doesn't crack or separate. Pour over the kebabs: bliss.

SLIGO

BLACKLION

CARLINGFORD

CROAGH
PATRICK

DUBLIN

IRELAND

PEEL

RAMSEY

DOUGLAS

ROA ISLAND

ISLE OF MAN

FLEETWOO

BLACKPOOL

Isle of Man & Ireland

HELLO FROM IRELAND

Morecambe Bay Potted Shrimps

SI: Dave and I were sat in the Bosun's Locker on Roa Island with tea and bacon sarnies.

'Kingy, have you ever been to the TT?'

'Nar, mate. I've always wanted to go, though. Have you?'

'I went when I was little with my dad, when the great Ron Haslam was still racing. Not much chance of getting there now, the ferries and hotels will be booked.'

'Ah, well, fancy another bacon sarnie, then?'

'Wait a minute, Kingy, I've got an idea!'

'This I've got to hear.'

'We've got our own boat . . .'

'Ye mean Pow Wow? You're a genius! When should we leave?'

It seemed like a good idea at the time. And if we were going half-way across the Irish Sea, why not go the whole hog and hit the Emerald Isle as well?

Pow Wow is Dave's catamaran. Known to the other members of the Roa Island Boat Club as 'the Rock 'n' Roll Bungalow', she's a fine boat and Dave an excellent skipper. In fact, they have several cups from the local regatta to prove it. But as visions of flame-haired barmaids bearing trays of the black stuff danced before our eyes, we didn't really stop to think this one through. We were going to sail to the Isle of Man and on to Ireland in Dave's boat. Sorted.

A week later, sitting in Dave's kitchen, we started to realise what we'd taken on. Sailing across the Irish Sea is no picnic at the best of times, and we were going to have to do it while cooking grub, being filmed, and swearing a lot less than we usually do when at sea. But there was an even bigger problem: how the hell were we going to get two motorbikes onto a 32-foot catamaran?

DAVE: The Isle of Man was always on our list. It has great food and the TT races. From Cumbria, where I live, it lies about sixty miles due west across the Irish Sea. Si and I both have our skipper qualifications, and old as *Pow Wow* is, we still race her and win…well, with the help of our mate Dave-the-Lifeboatman. Sailing across the Irish Sea to the TT races would also give us the opportunity to sample the seafood on the way. And with a mooring secured in the marina in Douglas just behind the beer tent, we would be in poll position to watch the races and have a wild time afterwards.

SI: Problem is, you can't go to the TT without a bike, and there was no way we could fit our usual tourers onto *Pow Wow*.

DAVE: The solution was to compromise: in this case our dignity and credibility, by agreeing to use two tiny Monkey Bikes. After a bit of research, though, we discovered that they've come on a bit. These days you can get them with racing engines, loud pipes, all the fancy bits, and they can cost up to £10,000 each. We contacted Monkey Bikes UK and managed to get a loan of two (we did, however, neglect to tell them how we proposed to get them to the Isle of Man). Mine had a race-tuned engine, loud pipes and a tartan seat – kind of like a Bay City Rollers memorial motorbike. The first time I got on it I dropped it into gear, did a wheelie and buried it in Si's kidneys. Si had the slightly larger bike called a 'Gorilla'. Well, if the cap fits…But what would the Mecca of motorcycling make of them? And of us?

SI: *'Kingy, do you think this bike looks a bit camp?'*

'Nar, looks all right to me, mate.'

'Ahhh, good. I was worried there for a minute!'

That's the great thing about asking your mate for his opinion: you can be confident of a truthful response.

DAVE: Getting the Monkey Bikes onto the catamaran was a hell of a job, but with the help of Chunky, another local lifeboatman, and a couple of knackering hours at low tide lifting and heaving, eventually they were stowed somewhere that still gave us a chance to eat and sleep. Chunky brought with him a key piece of news: we had one more glorious day ahead of us before things took a very nasty turn for the worse. The obvious thing to do would be to set off at first light, and race to the Isle of Man as fast as *Pow Wow* could manage. But there were two problems: first, we had to cook spring rolls, crab soufflés and fresh sea bass on board, and second, the 'glorious day' turned out to mean no wind. Not a breath. So we flapped and drifted away from Roa Island, and then dropped anchor and started cooking.

SI: The grey mullet round here is very good. Sometimes it's a muddy fish, because it crawls around silted-up harbours, but here it goes with the rip tide across Morecambe Bay and ends up sort of whirly-washed and hence a good, clean eat. We cooked our favourite spring rolls made with Morecambe Bay shrimp and tamarind, and made crab soufflés, which were a bit flat but very tasty. (I blame the offshore breeze cooling down the oven. What breeze? Ahem.) All this was washed down with a couple of bottles of pinot grigio and we decided to sleep that night on anchor and continue the next day.

We woke up with bangs coming from the galley as bottles fell off the shelves. The wind really had got up. After a quick call to Chunky at the lifeboat station we found a Force 8 was imminent and that the Isle of Man was a no-go – in fact the scary nautical phrase 'find a port of refuge' was used. So, with the sound and camera departments chucking up their ship's biscuits, we headed to Fleetwood. It was a horrendous ten miles, but we made it, battered, with bikes and crew intact. There was a slight snag about our arrival into Fleetwood: the rest of the film crew were waiting for us in Douglas.

'Hello, Belinda.'
'Hello lads, oh good, you're here.
I've got the beers in.'
'Ohhh good, but, well, we're not exactly with
you yet.'
'Oh. How far off are you – an hour or so?'
'Not exactly. Well, we, em … Ye see, we're in Fleetwood eating chips.'
'Fleetwood!'
'The weather turned and we had to make for the nearest port. We've still
got the cameraman and the sound supervisor, all safe. They're eating
chips – they're very nice, the chips here, ye know.'
'Will you STOP talking about CHIPS!'
'Sorry.'
'We'll have to get you on a ferry; God knows how I'm going to do that.'

Belinda rang back twenty minutes later with reservation numbers and a ferry time from Heysham. To this day we don't know what she had to promise to the management of the Steam Package Company. We stopped asking after a while, ye know; we didn't like to pry.

'And what a trip . . . grizzled Italians . . . mad-eyed Rammstein fans . . . motor-cross maniacs . . . not forgetting two large northerners on Monkey Bikes. But despite our differences, we all had several things in common: lack of sleep, exposure to various toxic foodstuffs from service stations, and a strong desire to get some ale down us before the ferry reached Douglas.'

Now, a bit about the TT: The Isle of Man TT (Tourist Trophy) Races are without doubt the best all-out road-racing motor-sport festival in the world. Attracting numerous teams and privateers, 12,000 bikes and upward of 40,000 spectators from all parts of the globe, it really is a must for anyone into bikes. The first races were in 1904, when the Automobile Club of Great Britain decided to hold the trials for the Gordon Bennett Challenge Cup on the island after the Manx government had changed the law to allow roads to be closed. In those days it was an event for cars only; the first motorcycle trials were held in 1905, but it was not till 1907 that the motorcycles had a race of their own. The Auto Cycle Club, a branch of the Automobile Club, wanted to use it as a way of promoting the efficient and cheap transport of motorcycling. The competitors were to complete 10 laps over 15 miles. These days, competitors race 6 laps of the 37-mile course with lap speeds of the top riders like John McGuiness reaching 127mph (the new lap record for 2005). Now that just sounds like facts and figures, but take a moment to think about it and you begin to realise the pedigree of this fantastic race. Then, when you get on your own bike and ride the course for yourself you soon realise how amazingly talented these guys are and the command they have over a motorcycle.

So, you get the vibe; you can see why we were desperate to go. There was no getting round it: we'd have to go on the ferry. And what a trip that was. Most of the 30,000 bikers headed for the TT seemed to be on the same ferry crossing as us: grizzled Italians with too-tight leathers, mad-eyed Rammstein fans from Düsseldorf, street racers, motor-cross maniacs, and every bike of every type imaginable. Not forgetting two large northerners on Monkey Bikes. But despite our differences, we all had several things in common: lack of sleep, exposure to various toxic foodstuffs from motorway service stations, and a strong desire to get some ale down us before the ferry reached Douglas. Fine sentiments, but not when combined with a Force 8 gale in the Irish Sea.

DAVE: We finally arrived only one day late. The buzz was great. I had last been there with my dad when I was eight years old, when Mike Hailwood and Phil Read were riding. I still treasure the autographs that I collected as a young boy. They were heroes with drum brakes. The bikes have changed but the people haven't.

SI: The first thing that hits you is the noise of thousands of bikes all hanging out on Douglas Prom, then the smell of bikes and fuel – nothing can beat that smell, you've just got to love it. Refreshment was needed, so a visit to Bushey's beer tent to pick up the vibe was a must, and of course a visit to, in our opinion, the best fish restaurant we've visited in a long time, the mighty Butch Buttery's Tan Rogan, which means 'king scallop' in Manx. Butch has a share in a fishing boat, and cooks whatever his boat catches. His menu is full of original ideas, and his fish is as it's meant to be: simple, fresh, and perfectly cooked.

Next morning, bright and early, we were off scouting the best vantage points to watch the racing. Then we visited the fairies at Fairy Bridge to ask for their blessing to get us round the course on Mad Sunday in one piece, a daunting prospect on two Monkey Bikes.

Ah yes, Mad Sunday: it can make even the biggest, baddest biker pause for thought. After a week of races, the course is opened up to all-comers. Which in this case meant us. We tried to point out to the director that tootling along at 45mph while superbikes hurtled past at about 130 was going to be . . . interesting. 'Good,' he said, 'I like interesting.' Secretly, though, we were looking forward to it with a weird mixture of excitement and terror.

Mad Sunday dawned grey and damp. If you were holed up in one of the remoter B&Bs on the island, and if you kept your window tightly closed and wore earplugs, you might have thought it was like any other June morning. But everywhere else, the air crackled with a mixture of noise, petrol and the unmistakable odour of 30,000 bikers who've been on the lash for a week. We set off from the grandstand to hoots of laughter and cheers of encouragement from the rest of the bikers. Dave did his usual grid start and I accelerated as quickly as I could without the front end of my Gorilla coming up to bite my nose off.

Soon it was the moment we had looked forward to: the mountain section. We were pleased that the police staggered the starts to give everyone a safe ride: we needed all the help we could get. The Monkey Bikes aren't fast by anyone's standards but are immense fun. We reached the dizzy speed of 65mph on a downhill bit, keeping to the extreme left-hand side to let the others pass us safely. Bikes passed like X-wing fighters at what felt like light speeds, and the noise was fantastic. There were some good riders, but dear me there were some bad ones as well. However, that's the good thing about being on a bike – we all should, and do in most part, look out for one another. So as long as you're not being an idiot, everything is cool and, more importantly, safe.

The craic with other bikers on the way round was great. Just being part of this historical spectacle was a fantastic feeling. If you ever get the chance to ride the course, take it; we highly recommend it. But a word of advice: leave your ego in the hotel or tent so you don't put yourself and other riders at risk. You'll enjoy the ride a lot more if you do.

GOOD LUCK
TO ALL WHO
VISIT THE FAIRIES

Betty-Jack

Fucidin!! 60

HAIRY
BIKERS
♡
LOVE
FAIRYS

NORTH EUSTON HOTEL

FOOD BITS

DAVE: We found the Manx people warm, helpful and passionate about their island and the food it produces. From scallops to lamb, crab to bread, everyone had an opinion on where we could get our hands on the best. It left us encouraged that the people are knowledgeable and care a great deal about the food they produce.

There are two significant native foods in the Isle of Man: the exquisitely sweet, marble-sized Manx scallops, or 'queenies', and the Loaghtan lamb, a unique prehistoric breed that cannot be beaten for flavour and texture. We hit both of these like a pair of sharks tucking into a shoal of mackerel. Si cooked one of the best things I have ever tasted: his tequila flambéed queenie scallops. We got a bucket of them from Tim Croft at Port St Mary, and they proved the adage 'small is beautiful': they were divine. The tequila thing wasn't just a biker gimmick; it worked really well. We had the nice dry tequila with lime and citrus, kind of like scallops with a margarita finish. Roll them up in a tasty wrap and enjoy.

The Loaghtan lamb is a strange and grumpy beast, which wanders aimlessly around the island – a bit like Si with a hangover. We went to visit George and Dianne Steriopulos who farm them. They are really weird to look at – I mean the sheep, not George and Dianne. They have four large horns that form an X sticking out from around their ears – a bit Dennis Wheatley. To farm them, you basically leave them well alone to let them thrive as they have done since dinosaurs roamed the Earth. When they need to gather them in, George and Dianne tempt them with ginger nuts – so they're a sort of self-marinating lamb. We met their prize ram, Bobbie Dazzler, who can service up to forty ladies at one time (I mean, that's even more than an average Cumbrian when he is full of Hartley's best bitter).

George and Dianne supply the lamb filleted or air-dried, a sort of magic Parma lamb. I asked George for the best way to cook a fillet. He said, 'As simply as possible, you need to do nowt.' Well, whilst delicious on its own, the lamb has plenty of flavour and can take a light marinade and some spices without being overshadowed, so, sort of ignoring him, I made lamb fajitas. They worked really well after Kingy's tequila scallops. Indeed, one of the posh bikers we fed, who was a sheep farmer, said it was a lot better than his own!

Another notable Manx favourite is the crab sandwich. At the harbour at Peel, bikers make a bee-line for the cafés and seafood sheds for this delight. It's simply bread, butter and good fresh crab, with lots of brown meat. Ooh, it's lovely with a pot of tea. The ice cream and cheeses are also good, and the Manx kippers are fantastic. You can have them posted anywhere in the world. There is also a distillery on the island at Glen Kella, which makes Manx whiskey, and very fine it is too. And there is fantastically good real ale from Bushey's and Oykell's. Beer is an old tradition on the island and, funnily enough, is a big player at TT week.

CRAB SOUFFLÉ

This is fab. It has quite robust flavours but the crab has enough of its own to carry them. It should be cooked on a rocking boat, under pressure, at your own risk!

Serves 6

30g butter, plus more to grease ramekins
2 tbs grated Parmesan cheese
30g flour
285ml milk
1 tbs tomato purée
½ tspn English mustard powder

a dash of tabasco
100g Gruyère, grated
1 dressed crab, brown and white meat
3 egg yolks
4 egg whites

Preheat the oven to 180°C. Then butter up 6 ramekin dishes and sprinkle with the grated Parmesan. Melt the 30g of butter in a pan and mix in the flour. Cook for a minute and gradually add the milk; yes, you are making a white sauce. When thickened, add the tomato purée, mustard and tabasco, then season. Add the Gruyère, taste again for seasoning, then add the crab.

When cooled slightly, add the slightly beaten egg yolks. Next, whip the egg whites till they are peaky, then fold gently into the mixture with a metal spoon. (Delia always mixes in a bit first, then gently, ever so gently, folds in the rest.) Pour the mixture into the ramekins.

Fill a roasting tin with an inch of water, then put the ramekins into this and the whole thing into the oven for 20 minutes, or until the soufflés are fully raised to a golden loveliness. Serve with salad and some warm country bread.

SEA BASS

With Lemon and Thyme Butter

There is in our opinion nothing better to eat than fresh fish fizzling with the taste of the ocean. This recipe is real easy and quick. If you decide to use whole fish, then rub some of the butter in the cavity before cooking.

Serves 4 hungry folk

125g unsalted butter, plus more to fry

zest of 1 lemon

1 tbs fresh thyme, chopped

8 fillets of sea bass, or 4 whole fish, gutted (you can also use grey mullet or any firm white fish)

juice of $\frac{1}{2}$ a lemon

1 clove garlic

olive or groundnut oil

In a bowl, put your butter, lemon zest, thyme and some salt and black pepper, and mash until all the ingredients have been absorbed into the butter. Set aside to let the flavours develop.

While the butter matures, melt a knob of butter with the oil over a medium heat, then fry the fillets until you achieve a light nutty-brown colour. Plate up and place one good knob of the flavoured butter on top of your fish. Serve with baby roast potatoes and a salad.

LIMED QUEEN SCALLOPS FLAMBÉED IN TEQUILA

Queen scallops are sweet gems from the coasts of the Isle of Man and they go brilliantly with lime and tequila – sort of queenie margaritas.

Serves 4 people

big dash of olive oil
big knob of butter
4 small shallots, finely chopped
juice of ½ a lime
zest of 1 lime

½ tspn sugar
about 40 queen scallops (or 20 king scallops)
good glug of quality tequila (you can drink the rest over dinner!)
handful of chives, finely chopped

Over a medium heat, in a heavy-bottomed frying pan, heat the olive oil and melt the butter. Sweat off your shallots (don't brown them!), add the lime juice and zest, and fry off for a minute or so. Add the sugar and stir. At this point it is important to keep the ingredients moving around the pan until such time as you add the scallops.

Increase the heat, add the queen scallops and fry for a further minute. Add a big glug of tequila and the chopped chives, then move the hot pan backwards and forwards over the flame to light the tequila – you know, Jamie Oliver and Gordon Ramsay stylie (but if you have an electric hob, ya goosed, so stand by with a naked flame of some sort – i've used a blowtorch before). Remove the scallops from the pan and serve in warm tortilla wraps or with lemon butter rice.

Just a note: if the tequila doesn't light quickly then don't be tempted to keep the pan on the heat. If you do you'll overcook the scallops and that's a BAD THING!

MORECAMBE BAY SHRIMP AND TAMARIND SPRING ROLLS

This is our signature dish and it is delicious. The little brown shrimps are brilliant with spring rolls, as their flavour is quite robust, but any prawns will do.

Makes either 6 large or 12 small

250g brown shrimps
100g beansprouts, chopped
1 stick of lemongrass, crushed and finely chopped (or use 3 tspns of preserved)
2cm of galangal, crushed and finely chopped (or use 1 tspn of preserved)
1 tbs soy sauce
$\frac{1}{2}$ tspn tamarind paste
1 tbs sake
1 red-hot chilli, seeded and finely chopped
1 tbs fresh coriander, chopped
$\frac{1}{2}$ tspn ground white pepper
1 packet of spring-roll wrappers
1 egg, beaten
groundnut oil

dipping sauce
2 garlic cloves, peeled and chopped
2cm of fresh ginger, peeled and chopped
2 chillies
1 tspn palm sugar
5 tbs lime juice
$1\frac{1}{2}$ tbs fish sauce

to serve
samphire
watercress

Combine the shrimps with the chopped beansprouts, then mix in the lemongrass and galangal. In a separate pot, soak the tamarind paste in the soy sauce for 20 minutes. Then add the sake and chilli and combine with the shrimp mixture. Add the coriander and the pepper, check the balance of flavours, and if it's too sharp add a bit of palm sugar. Then drain the mixture through a sieve so that it's not too wet, and you're ready to build your rolls.

So, take a spring-roll wrapper and wash with the beaten egg. Place a quantity of the shrimp mixture in the middle and roll up, à la Chinese carry-out. Don't overfill or it will end up like a *Doctor Who* monster. When you've made all your rolls, deep-fry them in the oil for about 5 minutes till golden.

For the dipping sauce, grind all the solid ingredients in a pestle and mortar and combine with the liquids – simple as that. Serve with the sauce you fancy, on a bed of samphire and watercress – God's salt and pepper.

MANX LAMB FAJITAS

A wok is good for this one. And as with the scallops, this is delicious wrapped in tortillas and served with guacamole, salsa and sour cream.

Serves 8

2 lamb fillets
2 tbs olive oil
2 tbs lime juice
1 tbs red-wine vinegar
3 cloves garlic, minced
1 tbs fresh oregano, chopped
a bunch fresh coriander, chopped

2 tspns ground cumin
$\frac{1}{2}$ tspn chilli powder
$\frac{1}{2}$ tspn paprika
1 green pepper, cut into thin strips
1 red pepper, cut into thin strips
1 onion, peeled and finely chopped

Cut the lamb into strips and combine everything in a bowl apart from the peppers and onion. Leave to marinate for a couple of hours, drain away the excess liquid and add the remaining ingredients. Fry it all off in a little hot corn oil for 5–10 minutes over a medium-high heat depending how pink you like your lamb.

Quick Guacamole

4 ripe avocados, roughly creamed
2 cloves of garlic, minced
$\frac{1}{2}$ tspn salt
juice of 1 lime
tabasco to taste

Whack all these ingredients together and enjoy! Can be garnished with a flourish of paprika and a spritz of lime zest.

Quick Salsa

3 juicy plum tomatoes, seeded
  and chopped
$\frac{1}{2}$ a green pepper, diced
2 tbs coriander, chopped

2 cloves garlic, finely chopped
couple of spring onions, chopped
2 tbs lime juice
1 tbs chopped jalapeno chilli

Mix it all up and season to taste. Leave to stand for at least 10 minutes for the flavours to meld.

DAVE: We landed in Ireland and were reunited with our BMWs. Ireland is lovely: a comfy country with comfy people. I felt ... well, like I was snuggling into a comfy duvet. There is great produce in Ireland, including, joking apart, the spuds. We went in search of the food and that mysterious enigmatic thing, the craic, which seems to be an interest in mutually beneficial conversation combined with the ability to talk confidently with strangers. With the craic you are never alone; I have never felt so welcome in a pub, café or street as I did in Ireland. The theme for our journey from east to west coasts was to find the top tips for the best Irish stew. But first the bikey bits.

SI: The roads in Ireland are much the same as those in the UK and the driving discipline is very good. A word of warning, though: the more rural you get the worse the roads become, and inevitably there is an increase in slow agricultural machinery and the odd bit of livestock sprinkled in for good measure. So take it easy – the last thing you want is to park your bike in the rear end of a horse; this does not make for good sightseeing, unless of course you're training to be a vet. Outside the main towns and cities, Ireland takes on a pace of its own – SLOW – so take a deep breath and ease yourself into it. You will get far more out of your trip if you just relax, take the weight off and appreciate the spectacular beauty that surrounds you.

FOOD BITS

Our first stop was a travellers' site, to ask the advice of folk who have been travelling through Ireland for generations. The travellers in Ireland have a tough life. They are not accepted as a minority and have to fight to keep their identity and lifestyle. We also met their priest, the amazing Father Stephen Monaghan. He prides himself on having the biggest parish in the whole of Ireland; indeed his parish *is* the whole of Ireland. He is a wonderful, caring man and gave us some top Irish-stew tips. Before we left, Maggie cooked us a whore's coddle, a hotchpotch of potato chowder with a cooked breakfast chucked in for good measure. It is great hangover food and set us in good stead for the trip north.

DAVE: Carlingford Lough is the best and most famous place in Ireland for oysters. Si adores them. I used to adore them, but got poisoned by one a few years ago. I sat all night in a bad way, seeing crustaceans snapping at my face whenever I shut my eyes. Now, when I eat oysters they make me a bit untidy, and each time it gets worse, so no oysters for Myers. With Kingy it's a different thing. He loves them and had a day in heaven. We filmed at an oyster farm run by a Dutchman, Peter Louet Fiesser, who arrived in Carlingford some twenty years ago on a catamaran with his wife and dog. Peter and his son Kian showed us the different types of oysters and how they are farmed. I was just window-shopping and felt like a pauper in Tiffany's. Eventually, we got our box of oysters, and, with our friend Brian, the owner of the Oystercatcher restaurant, headed for Carlingford Castle for the cooking.

Now, when you go travelling with Kingy, you know you're in the company of a man with not just a discerning palate, but a bloody great appetite to boot. There's usually at least one point on each trip where I and the rest of the crew can only sit back and look on in amazement as a week's shopping for a family of four disappears into his beard. What followed should probably have gone into the *Guinness Book of Records*. (Actually, the Guinness that followed should probably have gone in there as well.) As oyster after oyster disappeared into his gob, each one followed by an ecstatic 'Aw, man, Dave, that was a beauty!' I thought we were going to witness the return of Mr Creosote, the famous exploding gourmand at the end of Monty Python's *Meaning of Life*. I was trying to explain the finer delights of oyster po' boys whilst attempting to hang on to enough oysters to finish the dish. I reckon that Kingy and Brian got through four dozen. The only pleasure I had that day was a frugal gherkin sandwich.

SI: The only downside to the wonder that is the Carlingford oyster is that at some point you have to drink another pint of Guinness. Now that's all well and good, but your system builds up a bit of gas, so after you've put your leathers on and ridden 150km to the next stop, then taken your leathers off again, the smell that emanates is quiet unbelievable. Hey ho, never mind – a small price to pay, and it's only strangers that seem to mind.

The great thing about being on the road in Ireland is the pub lunch. It's an institution. When you arrive, a pint of water or cordial is immediately placed in front of you. Your lunch appears in minutes and it's good stuff: a starter, a choice of meats and vegetables, all fresh and cooked to perfection. Then, while you're tucking in, you can look around at the families, lads from the local building site, grandads with their grandchildren, office workers, farmers, groups of women of varying ages...all having lunch and a right laugh. As far as we could see, it was just another occasion for a community to come together over a great tradition.

DAVE: And if that's not enough, you're cajoled into having a pudding as well. A Mrs Doyle-like barmaid tries to tempt you. 'No,' we say. 'Go on!' she says. 'Go on. We've got a Malibu cheesecake with a Bounty topping, go on, it's lovely.' OK, we give in. Then a cheer goes up – the barmaids have been taking bets as to whether or not she could persuade us.

SI: We headed for Enniscrone in Sligo, and a bit of R&R – it's hard work, you know, eating your way through a country. We could not believe our luck: a seaweed bath! Oh, what joy; piping-hot sea water in a very large Victorian bath and lots and lots of seaweed, 'giving a feeling of complete well-being', or so the lady said as she handed over our towels. She was not wrong.

DAVE: On arrival you are shown to your room, a bath is drawn with the hot sea water, and a good bucketful or two of seaweed is thrown in. Whilst this is steeping you sit in the cedarwood steam cabinet being poached in clouds of sea water. When you are fully cooked you wobble over to the bath, your pores now open to receive all the iodine from the seaweed, and gently lower yourself into the primeval ooze. It feels strangely lovely, but it does pong a bit. After about an hour flitting from tub to steam cabinet and back, you pull a chain and are douched with ice-cold sea water. By heck, you do feel great – you could take on the world. Then, after you've dried off, you can sit in the foyer and have a cup of Irish tea. Heaven.

SI: We stayed in Ballina, Co. Mayo, that night, at Crockets on the Quay. Crockets serves great food and stout. They also do a fantastic breakfast and the lady that serves it is a wonderful character. We had sat down and she had served us with coffee. We eagerly awaited what promised to be a really good brekkie. We waited a bit longer and a bit longer. No sign of her. The next moment she came into the dining-room and announced, 'The Pope's dead, God rest his soul.' And that was that – not another word did she utter during breakfast, not even when asked for another round of toast. I hope she's spoken since.

From Ballina we headed for Belcarra with a purpose: we were trading in the bikes for a horse-drawn caravan. Now, you might think this a bit strange but what could be more relaxing than a traditional horse-drawn caravan? I had visions of us trundling gently along the lanes, Dave beavering away in the galley while I handled the driving in a cool but professional manner. Well, the pace was certainly gentle – somewhere between a trundle and a full stop, usually, with the latter more common than the former. Tommy, the horse, turned out to be a lot fonder of Dave's syllabub than he was of us, and after that we had a hard time getting him to stand up, never mind pull the caravan. Instead of lounging elegantly in the driving seat, reins held loosely in one hand and a cold tinny in the other, I found myself trudging along the road with Tommy on a short rein, trying to persuade him that two large Englishmen were just the sort of cargo a horse like him should be pulling. He was not convinced. Meanwhile, from the galley behind me, I could hear an impressive collection of oaths as another of Dave's creations rocked and rolled from worktop to floor. Our new stress-free environment turned out to be anything but, and after a couple of days it was a great relief to get back on a machine that went forward when you told it to without arguing.

DAVE: In Belcarra there is a jewel in the shape of a drinking establishment and B&B called Flukie's Cosy Bar, run and owned by Flukie, surprisingly enough, and his fantastic wife, Geraldine. We just wanted a quick fruit juice and a pee. We left two hours later, not because we were drinking or eating but because we got stuck in with the craic. We met the regulars, Gerry and Mr Magoo and all, and the pub became our base for a part of the filming.

SI: We have never had a welcome like it; all the regulars in the bar were fantastic characters, full of fun, interest and courtesy. The word was out that a ceildih was planned on the Friday night and was not to be missed, so we stayed on to join in. There were some amazing musicians playing and the drink and craic was flowing thick and fast, as only it can in Ireland. At one point in the evening there was a Swedish woman in the middle of the floor giving it what-for – I'm never likely to see legs jig like that again – and a fella trying to flog his sheep to whoever would listen.

DAVE: It was the end of our journey, and we were finally ready for our Irish stew cook-off. I put together all the tips and information we had gathered on the road to make a refined, posh version, the ultimate Irish stew – the Bistro Bonanza. I took the finest ingredients and blended my spices with the skill of Rembrandt mixing his paint. Kingy, however, decided he would go minimal (yes, he was taking the cuisine back to the potato famine). As my perfect chump chops were delicately placed in even layers with Virgonian precision, Kingy plopped in his bits of scrag end. His vegetables were chucked in like shrapnel; mine joined the dish like the chorus of *Swan Lake* entering stage-right. Anyway, enough of this; I have to say the end result was two very passable Irish stews.

SI: The trip was full of good memories: Myers and Dave Rea, our cameraman, tunefully serenading the locals with karaoke in Carlingford; Flukie's Bar in Belcarra, with the best fiddle band you'll hear in your life; proper pub lunches, where people really do put work aside for an hour to enjoy life (and decent helpings). Is this what is meant by the craic? We weren't sure – but we had a damn good time trying to find out.

OYSTERS AU NATUREL

Get the freshest oysters you can, shuck and serve with lemon and maybe Worcestershire sauce, Tabasco or the traditional red-wine vinegar and shallot dressing.

OYSTERS PO' BOYS

This is the butty from heaven. The recipe is a three-parter, and it can take a while to shuck 24 oysters if you're not practised…The cornmeal crust on the oysters gives a fab texture and flavour, and it also instantly seals the oyster, so it cooks lightly in its own juices and none of the fat is absorbed – it's like a crispy, tasty, self-engaging pressure cooker. We use grapeseed oil to fry them as its flavour is really pure.

The remoulade

This is the ultimate tartare-cum-seafood sauce – it's got the lot. And any leftovers are great with your fish-finger sandwiches.

Serves 4

1 small jar mayonnaise, or make your own
1 tbs fresh tarragon, chopped
1 tbs capers
1 tbs shallots, finely chopped
1 tspn French mustard
a dash of Tabasco

1 tbs tomato paste
2 tbs lemon juice
1 tspn red-wine vinegar
$\frac{1}{2}$ tspn cayenne pepper
1 tbs horseradish sauce

Simply mix together and adjust to taste.

For the cornmeal crust

140g cornmeal
1 tbs ground cumin
1 tspn ground fennel
1 tspn cayenne pepper

Mix and season to taste.

Assembling the masterpiece

2 dozen small oysters, shucked
1 egg and 3 tbs milk, beaten
grapeseed oil

to serve
French bread, warmed
crispy lettuce

Dry the freshly shucked oysters, dip into the egg wash, coat liberally with the cornmeal mixture, and deep-fry in the oil till golden – 1 to 2 minutes.

Next, take the French stick, split it and butter one side. Then put on it a layer of crispy lettuce, a layer of the remoulade sauce, then the crisp oysters. Cover with the other half and tuck in.

IRISH STEW: MUM'S VERSION

Traditionally, Irish stew is a white stew of lamb, potatoes and very little else. Here's our take on it. Thick neck chops from the butcher would be best, as would some good liquid lamb stock (no, not cubes) if you haven't got your own. And to get the best possible flavours out of the minimum of ingredients, use the best seasonings you can find – it will be worth it.

Serves 4

a good glug of oil
a big knob of butter
4 medium onions, peeled and cut into various sizes
3 cloves garlic, peeled and crushed

6 large potatoes, peeled and cut into various sizes
8 lamb chops
565ml lamb stock
parsley (optional)

In a large pan, heat the oil and butter. Sweat off the onions and garlic, slowly teasing the flavours out – 15 minutes or so over a low heat should do it. Add the potatoes and cover them in the creamy juice of the onions and garlic. Add lots of freshly ground black pepper and 3 pinches of salt (2 pinches if you've got big hands). Leave the potatoes and onions in the pan for a further 15 minutes over a very low heat, making sure you don't burn them. If you are worried they may burn, then add a little bit of stock.

Now attend to the lamb: trim the fat off the chops and place it in a frying pan over a low heat. Let the fat render down, then add salt and pepper. Remove from the frying pan what remains of the solid fatty bits, then add your chops. Once brown, remove and place them in the pan with the onions and potatoes.

Add some of the stock to the frying pan to get all the nice, savoury, jammy bits off the bottom, then add to your chops, onions and potatoes. Pour the remainder of the stock into the pan, to just below the level of your ingredients. Put the lid on and leave for 1½ hours over a low heat. Should your heart desire, add some parsley 10 minutes before the stew is ready. Remove it from the heat and leave for about 10 minutes to rest. Taste and adjust seasoning.

How simple is that?

IRISH STEW: BISTRO BONANZA

Simple's great, but using some of the top tips we were given on our travels around Ireland, we added Guinness, barley and herbs to make this a special occasion stew.

Serves 6

12 good lamb chops, sliced thinly
2 carrots, peeled and diced
2 parsnips, peeled and diced
1 small swede, peeled and diced
1 large onion, peeled and sliced
1kg good floury potatoes, peeled and sliced
a couple of sprigs of thyme
a sprig of rosemary

2 tbs parsley (the old-fashioned curly stuff), chopped
1 bay leaf
a handful of barley
500ml rich stock
500ml Guinness
a big knob of butter

Preheat the oven to 150°C.

Trim most of the fat off the meat, and render it down in a frying pan. In this fat, brown the chops and set aside. In the same frying pan, heat a little olive oil, then brown the carrots, parsnips, swede and onion. Set aside the veg, and start building your stew. First grease a big pan, then put a layer of potatoes, then a layer of half of the veg, then season. Add the chops and herbs, season again; add the barley, then more potatoes (but save some for the top) and the final layer of veg. Season for a final time, then arrange the final spuds in a nice pattern on the top and dot with butter. Pour over the stock and Guinness, cover and bake in the oven for about 2½ hours, occasionally skimming any fat off the surface. Then you can then either take the lid off for another half an hour to brown the top, or cheat and put it under the grill. The spuds should vary between crispy on the top to chowder-like by the time you get to the bottom.

Serve with colcannon.

COLCANNON

A fantastic stand-alone vegetarian dish but, crikey, it's good with a couple of rashers of bacon and a fried egg…

Serves 4–6

Spring cabbage will do, but we think
 kale is better.
400g kale
1kg floury spuds, peeled

2 shallots, peeled and finely chopped
1 tbs chives, chopped
140ml cream
125g butter

Cut the tough stems out of the kale, boil until tender, then chop into slices. Boil the spuds in salted water and mash. Meanwhile, simmer the shallots and chives in the cream for about 5 minutes. Mix everything together, season well, and then, if your arteries can stand it, top with a puddle of melted butter – mmmm…

WHORE'S CODDLE

This is a bit like an all-in-one breakfast stew – the ultimate morning-after-the-night-before hangover cure.

Serves 6

2 large onions, peeled and sliced
8 thick rashers of bacon
6 large pork sausages, cut into chunks
1kg potatoes, peeled and sliced
285ml stock
4 tbs parsley, finely chopped

In a large pan, layer the onions, bacon, sausage and potatoes, then add the stock. Season, cover and simmer for about 1½ hours till the spuds have broken down. Add the parsley and stir so that the broken-down potatoes thicken the liquid. Serve with soda bread and, well…maybe a small Guinness.

BOXTY

These can be sweet or savoury. A good compromise is to serve them with strips of crispy bacon and maple syrup for breakfast. Gorgeous.

Serves 6

500g potatoes, peeled and grated
500g cold mashed potato
450g plain flour
1 heaped tspn baking powder
a large knob of butter, melted
200ml milk

Squeeze the raw potato through a tea towel to get rid of any liquid, and mix with the mashed potato. Add the flour, baking powder and the melted butter and season to taste. Now, depending on whether you want your boxty to be like a cake or like a drop scone, add the milk to suit. For a breakfast pancake, add the milk till it goes like a heavy batter, drop blobs of it into hot oil and fry till golden.

IRISH WHISKEY SYLLABUB

This is lovely served with shortbread fingers or a nice brandy snap. If it's left to chill for a while it will separate a bit, but we like it like this, so don't start trying to rebuild it. Whiskey glasses are ideal to serve it in.

Serves 6

juice and zest of 1 lemon
6 tbs runny honey
8 tbs Irish whiskey
500ml heavy double cream
freshly grated nutmeg

Combine the first three ingredients (at this stage it looks a bit like a cold cure). Add the cream, whip till it starts to thicken, then spoon into glasses. Top with grated nutmeg and chill for 1 hour.

HUNGARY

MARMURES

SIGHISOARA

ROMANIA

TÂRGU-JIU

BUCHAREST

SERBIA &
MONTENEGRO

BULGARIA

Transylvania

SI: Imagine you're in charge of tourism in an ex-Eastern Bloc country. After years of suffering under a particularly brutal communist regime, you're struggling to show the world what a great tourist destination your country could be. With only one building that is internationally recognisable, it's not easy; but what's this? A couple of big lads from the BBC, eager to tell the world about your country, and especially all the great food they're bound to find? Could you let them join a tour of camcorder-wielding tourists and film in the Palace of Parliament?

Course you couldn't.

And there, in a nutshell, is the Great Romanian Contradiction: a vibrant, energetic country full of delights, but one that still struggles to shake off some aspects of its Soviet-dominated past. Thankfully, the jobsworth at the Ministry of Tourism was our first and last encounter with the type of bureaucracy that used to strangle the place, but Romania is still a country in transition. And what's driving the changes are some of the most interesting people we met anywhere on our travels.

There's no doubt we'd arrived full of misconceptions about the place. For some reason we'd imagined a grey, concrete wasteland, possibly populated by surly Slavic gangsters and suspicious families nervously ushering their children away from these two large embodiments of capitalist excess. The reality was utterly different. Romania is, as the name suggests, a Latin country; the people are dynamic, colourful and welcoming. And once you get away from the, admittedly hideous, steelworks and chemical factories, you find yourself in one of Europe's last great wildernesses. They even have wolves, wild boar and bears, for God's sake – brilliant!

Transylvania is, of course, just one part of Romania, the big central region of about 100,000 square kilometres, and we were dying to explore it on the bikes. Not just because it's a stunningly beautiful place, but because the name instantly conjures up scary forests, bulbs of garlic, and two little puncture marks in the neck. Like everyone who's grown up watching Hammer horror films, we wanted to know more about the real story of Dracula. Preferably without actually meeting him.

A BRIEF AND INCOMPLETE
HISTORY OF ROMANIA

DAVE: Romania borders Bulgaria, Serbia, Hungary, Ukraine, Moldavia and the Black Sea. So, politically you have this massive melting pot with constantly changing borders and influences. Before Christ, Romania was mainly tribal, with a brief Dacian Empire occupying the territory from about 50 BC. The Romans came and conquered between AD 87 and 106, and the area prospered. They had left by the fifth century, at which point various nomadic people – the Huns, Avars, Slavs and Bulgars – swept into the the lowlands.

The Carpathian Mountains protected the Daco-Romanian community to some extent, although the Magyars claim that present-day Transylvanians are from Slavic stock. Indeed there are a lot of blonde, blue-eyed folk there. I like the story that they are the descendants of the children that followed the Pied Piper into the mountainside, then emerged in Transylvania on the other side.

In the fifteenth century, the great patriot Vlad Tepes, or 'Vlad the Impaler', brought a kind of stability. Son of Vlad Dracul, he was one of the inspirations for Bram Stoker's Dracula, but if anything his story is even more blood-thirsty. He was born in 1431 and, after a career fighting the Turks with legendary cruelty, came to power in 1456. To consolidate that power he bought off the very enemies that had previously buried his father and brother alive. His method of law enforcement was simple: practically all crimes were punishable by death. His favourite method of execution was to have the victims spread-eagled and a stake hammered up their rectum. They were then raised aloft and left to die in agony. After one battle he is reported to have impaled 20,000 people in a vast forest of stakes, after which he felt the urge to dine in the midst of this carnage. As impaling caught on, Vlad built a machine to do it more efficiently. This charming relic is now in a museum and is thankfully redundant.

Another notorious incident occurred in Walachia, where he invited all the beggars, disabled and work-shy to a banquet. He asked them whether they wanted to be relieved of life's sufferings, then, after the predictable response, set fire to the building and burnt them to death. Thus were his social problems solved and the phrase 'a beggars' banquet' born. (Was this the beginning of Thatcherite social policy, one wonders?) On another occasion, a party of Turkish dignitaries refused to remove their headgear for religious reasons, so Vlad simply nailed their hats to their heads. (What a great way to persuade a teenager to remove their baseball cap!) Once, when arguing with a mistress about whether or not she was pregnant, he cut her stomach open to prove she wasn't. Well, she was, but it was a bit late by then.

Thankfully, he was murdered by a servant in 1476, though whether he was given the same treatment as his many victims is not recorded. After this particularly gruesome period, Romania was swallowed up by the Ottoman Empire and remained under its rule until the empire's demise in the nineteenth century. After the Second World War, Romania became a communist state, under Soviet control, until its next great despot arrived on the scene.

Nicolae Ceausescu came to power in 1965 and at first was a popular ruler (although worryingly he once called Vlad the Impaler 'a fighter for independence and a wise law-maker'). But his policies of heavy industrialisation slowly drove the Romanians into greater and greater poverty. Huge Golgothic factories were built in the face of architectural treasures, as if to put two fingers up at their cultural heritage. In 1966, to increase his workforce, he banned abortions and contraception for any woman under forty who had fewer than four children. In the 1980s he introduced the 'baby police', who could force a woman to have a gynaecological examination. The result was many children being abandoned in state orphanages.

Abuses of human rights became worse throughout the 1980s, with camps being set up all over Romania. Up to one in four of the population was accused of being an informer, arrested and effectively sentenced to an early death. We visited one camp at Sighet, on the Ukrainian border, which is now a museum for victims of communist oppression. There are thousands of photos of the people who died at the prison, including priests, children and your average granny, all there simply because they were rumoured to have criticised the regime. The place smelled of death and made us all realise how much we take free speech for granted. We also saw pictures of Ceausescu with lots of world leaders, including the British royal family and President Nixon – lots of nice handshakes and smiles.

Ceausescu's palace is the most visible evidence of his megalomania. The Palace of Parliament, or the People's Palace as it is now known, is the second largest building in the world after the Pentagon. To the locals it's known as the Madman's House. We tried to get permission to film inside, but it was a non-starter due to the bureaucracy and the huge cost, although it probably didn't help that the Secret Service are still ensconced in the basement. We did, however, film a cookery item on the roof of the tax office, which gave us an amazing view of the building. It is twelve storeys high and has four storeys underground, including a nuclear bunker. There are 1,100 rooms, 4,500 chandeliers, and at one time 700 architects worked on the project. Churches, houses and even a hill were removed to enable its construction. The end result is really tacky, like a mega-giant stone-clad council house. I rejoice in the fact that the first person to appear on the balcony after the revolution was Michael Jackson, who apparently turned to the crowds and passionately proclaimed: 'I love Budapest!' Oops.

Not surprisingly, the people were eventually driven to revolt. At the end of 1989, in a three-day uprising, Ceausescu was overthrown and quickly executed. Since then the country has been slowly emerging from its communist past. We really noticed the energy and optimism of its people. They have seized their freedom, and with a lot of hard work are slowly building a new country.

DAVE: Our journey started in the capital, Bucharest. It's a busy, bustling city, much of it a mess, but its boulevards and markets are vibrant and fun. Before setting out on the trip we'd managed to blag an interview with Romania's current best-known export, the Cheeky Girls (purely in the interest of gastronomic research, as Si explained to his missus). And it was from the Cheekies that we heard about gogosi, a kind of fast-food doughnut that is sold all over the city. 'Fills a corner nicely,' said Si, sticking another half dozen away.

Leading west from Bucharest is Romania's only bit of motorway. Actually, motorway is probably pitching it a bit high, and anyway, after 100km the autostrada just stops and you're faced with a seasonal hazard, the haycart. 'Wow, look at that – that's so cool,' said Wavey Davey, our production assistant, snapping away at the horse and laden cart as it passed.

An hour later, as the four-hundredth similar cart lumbered into view, even Wavey's legendary enthusiasm had waned. Trying to get to Târgu Jiu by nightfall was proving difficult, especially as every farmer in Walachia seemed to have decided this was the day to get the hay in.

Târgu Jiu was the birthplace of Romania's greatest sculptor, Constantin Brancusi. After the First World War, the women of the town commissioned the most amazing piece of modern art as a war memorial. It is an installation that takes you on a walk through the town, following the soldier's life from cradle to grave. You start at the river, which represents life, move to his Table of Silence, which represents the passage of time, walk through the Avenue of Stools, representing the soldier's working life, then through the Gate of the Kiss. You eventually end up at Brancusi's masterpiece, the Infinite Column, which Si named the Stairway to Heaven. Standing some thirty metres high, it really is awesome; you will have a lump in your throat.

SI: Dave was particularly keen to see the Gate of the Kiss, and not just for artistic reasons. Apparently, if you toss a coin clean over the impressive arch, good fortune will shine on your love life. Dave's coin landed on the top and stayed there.

As we reached the spectacular castle at Hunedoara it became very, very hot. We set up our table near the drawbridge, and while the sarmales steamed away on the stove, we began to sweat like James Brown in a sauna. And then, from below, came the sound of girls playing in a waterfall, splashing cool water from the moat over each other. It was slowly dawning on us that Romanian women are, in fact, the most beautiful in the world. In Bucharest we almost came off our bikes around every corner as another gorgeous face appeared. So only the excellent smell coming from the pan stopped me from tearing my clothes off and joining them.

By the time we'd finished, we were desperate for a swim, and finding out that there was a spa on our route seemed like a real stroke of luck. But then, of course, the word 'spa' covers many things. And one of the things it covers (in Romania) is a former open-cast salt-mine, now filled with stinking black mud and large Romanian matrons. Kitted out with a pair of dodgy Soviet Speedos that made us look like a cross between Mick and Michelle McManus, we were poked and provoked by the crew into smearing ourselves with muck. And while they wept with laughter, Stroudie the director says, 'Why don't you try and chat up those two women over there?' The resulting scene was too painful to broadcast, even by our own unusually flexible standards. And hopefully, the ladies will both be out of therapy and on the road to recovery in a year or so...

DAVE: Our next stop was Sighisoara, the cultural capital of Transylvania. We arrived as the annual Medieval Festival was in full swing. Teenagers from all over Romania seemed to have made a kind of Goth-pilgrimage to the event, scattering clouds of white foundation and black eyeliner in their wake, while the older attendees picked through the bargains on the jewellery and handicraft stalls. Sighisoara itself is a stunning town, dominated by its massive medieval clock tower, and ringed with Saxon ramparts and battlements. At its heart is the birthplace of Dracula himself: Vlad the Impaler.

Actually, when Bram Stoker wrote his novel *Dracula* in 1897 (without ever having set foot in Transylvania), he drew on several sources and legends. There was the infamous Hungarian Countess, Elizabeth Bathory, who tortured and drained the blood of over 600 young women in her quest for an original anti-ageing formula. There were the many stories and legends of vampires throughout Eastern Europe – tales of the undead, doomed to rise from their graves and walk the Earth in search of further victims. And then there was Vlad the Impaler. Standing outside his birthplace while folk bands played and clowns cavorted, it was still possible to feel a strange chill down the back of one's neck...

We believe the best solution to a nasty experience is lunch. We'd booked a table at the Casa cu Cerb, a lovely hotel on the corner of the square, and were surprised to be greeted in the lobby by a large signed photo of Prince Charles. What was he doing here? While we tucked into some mighty fine deer goulash soup, we found out from the staff that he'd long taken a low-key interest in the area, and particularly its Saxon history (he is a Saxe-Coburg, after all). He was particularly fond of a chicken-noodle soup made locally. Being food detectives, we were intrigued: could we sample Prince Charles's favourite soup? We asked for more information and everyone went quiet except for a lovable cleaning lady who told us that it was made by her friend Sara in the village of Viscri.

Viscri is an old Saxon citadel about 30km from Sighisoara, and is typical of villages in the area. Sara is a further 12km down a dirt track. Which is how we found ourselves in a tiny piece of paradise: a small kitchen garden, full of the most wonderful vegetables, next to a yard full of chickens, a well, a friendly pig in a sty, all presided over by an extraordinary woman. Sara is the kind of granny everyone would want: warm, funny and with a gentle energy that keeps her smallholding buzzing with activity. As the horses clopped past and the bees hummed in the vines above the windows, Sara poured us another glass of her home-made tuica (a kind of synapse-snapping plum brandy), and Kingy had the look of a man who'd won the lottery and pulled Elle Macpherson in the same afternoon.

Sara's chicken-noodle soup turned out to be the most comprehensively home-made food I have ever had. The chicken was one of her own, the water was from her well, the noodles were home-made and all the vegetables were home-grown. It was a thing of simple loveliness, and her pride in it glowed through every mouthful. We looked at pictures of Sara with Prince Charles (we felt maybe we were intruding on the man's private life) and our respect for the prince grew as we realised how well liked he is in the village and how much he appreciates this idyllic, simple life. We in turn were honoured to be able to cook Sara chicken paprikas with lemon spaetzles. As she ate our food on the sunny Transylvanian hillside and we enjoyed a glass of good Romanian red, she told us that we made her feel like Lady Di or Camilla. Well, Sara, you will always be our queen.

That evening, we ate with the crew in a nearby farmyard lit by a bulb dangling from the tree above us. The animals wandered past into their stalls for the night, and the farmer and his wife served up plate after plate of delicious local produce until we could hardly move. Life really doesn't get much better than days like this.

SI: The final leg of our trip was into the very north of Romania. Maramures is another traditional farming region, right up by the Ukrainian border, and is a stunning place. All along the roadside, families were building haystacks, the children perched perilously on top while the parents heaved fork after fork of hay in their direction. The farms and churches are almost all wooden, and fronted by enormous roofed gateways; the bigger the gates, the better your standing in the community. Built into these gates often are benches, where the older members of the family will sit in the evening light and watch the world go by – or in this case, two large Englishmen with bug-spattered glasses.

We'd heard about the 'Merry Cemetery' at Sapanta, but had no idea what to expect. 'What's next, the Jolly Crematorium?' pondered Dave. But what we found was not only stunning, but somehow summed up our whole experience of the Romanians we'd met. Each headstone is made of wood, carved by a local artist, Dumitru Pop, a delightful bloke who chiselled away at his next commission while explaining his work. The deceased's memorial is then painted in bright primary colours, with a picture of their life or how they died, and an inscription telling passers-by something of their story. Instead of gloomy gravestones with mournful mottoes, you get a celebration of life: colourful, vivid, plain-spoken. Rather wonderful, and very Romanian.

Our final night was spent in a small hotel in Cluj, awaiting an early flight back to Bucharest the next morning. The last night, or 'wrap', of a shoot is always a good opportunity for a little bevvy or two, and the evening was proceeding nicely towards its civilised conclusion when someone remembered a gift we'd been given in Transylvania: a 1-litre Coke bottle filled with a particularly lethal home-made tuica. We repaired to my room – and that's about all I can remember of that evening. I awoke at 4 a.m. to hear Belinda, our line producer, outside my door arguing furiously with the hotel's grumpy owner, who was determined to check the contents of my minibar before we departed. 'There's no point,' reasoned Belinda, 'there's nothing left in it.' She was right, too. Which is why the 06.35 flight from Cluj to Bucharest took off with a strange group of people all wearing dark glasses and saying very little.

BIKE BITS

SI: In Bucharest we had picked up a BMW GS1200 and a BMW 650F. Collecting my kids from school six months prior to the trip, I had spoken with a lorry driver who had driven to Romania to deliver shoe boxes full of goodies to the orphanages there. I told him of the trip we hoped to make and a furrow formed across his brow. 'Hope you lads have got good insurance, then.' He went on to describe the driving attitude and the road surfaces in Romania as only a trucker could: very bad indeed. 'Listen, mate, it's bad enough in a 40-tonne truck. Gawd knows what it would be like on a bike – they drive like loonies out there.'

Well, I thought, ye know what truckers are like. It can't be that bad! Ohhhh how wrong I was. Biking in Romania is a blood sport, sort of equivalent to running the wrong way up the M1 blindfolded. What they lack in road rage they make up for in an almost psychotic desire to overtake in the most unpredictable and dangerous manner possible. And if you're a bike coming in the other direction – tough. But it is also fun, rewarding, challenging (sometimes downright nuts), and I think it's safe to say that neither Dave nor I would change any of the experiences we had on those roads.

The first thing you notice when you're riding a bike in Romania is that other road users give you no quarter at all. In fact the overwhelming consensus seems to be that you're a pain in the arse and should join the dark side and buy a car. Driving attitudes generally are dangerous and macho, in part due to the poor road infrastructure and therefore high frustration levels, but also a Latin temperament that is far in excess of any Italian I've ever met. The men tend to drive, and if a biker happens to overtake them it seems to be taken as a declaration of war and all rules go out the window.

Due to the single-carriageway roads that wind through the country and are used by every conceivable form of vehicle, overtaking is an interesting necessity. In fact it has become an art form, and goes something like this: when you feel like it, you go for it, no matter what is coming the other way, the general idea being that oncoming drivers don't want to die so they'll get out of your way. That's all well and good for a 40-tonne truck; however, you're a tad more vulnerable on a bike, and that, coupled with the apparent prevailing attitude of other road users – that bikes are the devil's work – makes for some interesting riding and some varied hand gestures.

In the cities and large towns, the surfaces of the roads are worn, and for years have been soaked in diesel so are very, very slippy, even when dry. It gets better as the summer wears on and the dust builds up, but then the authorities wet the inside lanes slightly to keep the dust down, so it becomes like riding through an oil-slick: the front end of the bike wants to take you for a salsa lesson and the back end wants to waltz, so you end up with everything clenched to within an inch of its life.

As ever, there are exceptions to every rule. One person we met was anything but macho; in fact Cristi the bike-builder was probably the most passionate and interesting bike-man we have ever met. As a fellow member of the biking fraternity, he quickly asked if we'd mind coming to see a bike he'd been working on for the past four years. It was a thing of absolute beauty: a chrome-dressed Ural chopper built, from the tyres up, by hand.

Now, you may think this is no real shakes, but you must take into consideration the economic climate in Romania and the complete lack of financial resources that this man had at his disposal. This wonderful machine was a labour of love that had had many, many hours of care and attention bestowed on its design and build. Even Dave was impressed, and choppers don't really light his candle. The engine was a 650 Ural thumper (which happened to be Dave's first bike), and the frame, exhausts, wiring loom, seat, bars, cables, shockers, wheels, oil tank and foot pegs were all either handmade or adapted to fit from car, van, lorry or tractor parts. The brakes, for instance, were from a Dacia car and had been hand-polished, like most other shiny bits, for the bike.

From when I was very small I have had a great love for choppers; they strike a chord with me because most of the time they are designed and built with a little bit of the owner's personality and love in them. That's why Dave and I had such respect for Cristi; we both understood the effort, time, scrimping and saving that he had had to do to realise his dream.

'In fact we would advise not to travel at night, particularly in the summer months, as horses and carts tend to be on the roads late into the evening, bringing in the harvest.'

I can still remember the moment he turned to me with a big smile and said, 'Do you want to ride?' I have never had my leg over something so quick in my life, although others may disagree. The engine rumbled into life, the exhaust note sounding like a Lancaster bomber, and we were off. She rode so well, I could tell that as well as being a great guy, Cristi really did know his onions. And having handed over his pride and joy to some mad Geordie he'd just met, he wouldn't take a cent for his trouble. It was the highlight of my trip and an opportunity for us to marvel at the commitment of one man to produce such a great bike against all the odds. Thanks, Cristi – if there was one person who epitomised Romanian friendliness, it was you.

As you head north, the road surfaces seem to get better, but don't allow me to lull you into a false sense of security; you need to keep a keen eye out for potential roadworks as there is little or no advance warning, and the contractors have a tendency to plane miles and miles off the surface of the road, then leave it for a few months. So not only must you contend with a deeply rutted surface, but huge potholes and, in some areas, complete collapse.

It is very important that you ride with your documentation; you will be stopped by traffic police, if for no other reason than to have a good look at your bike. Carrying your documentation saves you a lot of hassle and hours in a local police station standing in a queue the length of the M6. They also have a tendency to stop you at night, just out of town, at the darkest part of the road, so all that's visible are the reflective strips on the small baton they wave in the air and as a result ye breakfast nearly ends up in your leathers.

In fact we would advise not to travel at night, particularly in the summer months, as horses and carts tend to be on the roads late into the evening, bringing in the harvest. We had occasion to ride at night through a very rural area, and happened rather suddenly upon one cart laden with hay, moving very slowly, without lights. We, on the other hand, were moving quite quickly with lights. The only reason we saw this lumbering pile of horse and hay were the sparks from the horse's hooves scraping the tarmac. Evasive action was taken and we avoided parking our bikes in the horse's backside.

I don't mean to give the wrong impression about touring in Romania. The country is stunning and its people warm and courteous. And some roads are quite good, so should the opportunity arise, you would be bonkers not to go. All we are saying is, have some touring experience under your wheels first. It really isn't for the inexperienced or faint-hearted.

FOOD BITS

DAVE: Now, on to the food. Start with a good Mediterranean foundation, throw in some Turkish influences (the tripe soup, dolmas and aubergine purée), a dash of Hungarian (goulash and monster biscuits), and a bit of Russian for good measure and you have the mix that gives us a really fine, interesting cuisine. We liked Romanian food, although sometimes it was a bit much for my delicate palette. But Kingy worked very well on a diet of tripe soup, mititei and a slab of lard on the side. Wash that down with a gallon of Romanian beer and you end up with a kind of active volcano with a gurgling smile. The strongest Turkish influence is in Bucharest, with tripe soup being endemic in both countries. (I preferred the pork version as the tripe one frankly smells of piss.) They also have fabulous dolmas, stuffed with chicken and dill. Then you move on to the more robust sarmale, or stuffed cabbage rolls. Our recipe, with speck and disgruntled German (sauerkraut), is the best. There is a fine patisserie in Bucharest too, with a strong Austrian vibe. A quick waltz or a Mozart ball is not hard to find.

As you head to the Danube delta you get a lot of carp, or 'crap' as it is in Romanian – honest! ('Oooh, thank you, miss, I'll have some of your lovely crap…So long as it's fresh.') The basic road-food is mititei (meaning 'little ones' and pronounced 'meech'). These are small skinless sausages full of spices and paprika. They are also full of bicarbonate of soda to give them a bouncy texture. I don't like this, as you can taste the bicarb and it makes you fart like a badger. Our recipe uses a bit of baking powder, which works well on the texture front but also ensures you don't get sent to Coventry. At roadside cafés you order maybe half a dozen of these with a pot of Dijon mustard. Very tasty. As you pass through the Carpathian Mountains the food changes again and you get a more Hungarian influence, with goulash and paprikas (pronounced 'paprikash') creeping in. We also found freshly baked spicy biscuits the size of drainpipes.

As we journeyed north there were yet more food revelations. When you've sat in a hotel in Sibiu once frequented by Liszt and Strauss, eating finest Beluga with bone spoons, some crispy toast and glasses of iced vodka, you begin to see what all the fuss over caviar is about. At the other end of the spectrum, we discovered balmos, a kind of porridge favoured by

> 'Romania was a great surprise. We expected a dull
> post-communist country with little to recommend it. We got
> a colourful, cultured country full of warmth and hospitality.
> Romanians truly have heart and soul.'

Romanian shepherds. It is a mixture of young cheese, mamaliga (polenta) and butter. It's heavy, very heavy; in fact you could lag pipes with it. It is, though, very tasty and something we wanted to try to cook ourselves.

We were going to film some shepherds making it in the hills, but got up on the appointed day to find the road washed away by heavy rain. Undeterred, we asked around and were given the address of a lady called Maria near the Ukrainian border who would cook us balmos instead. She was dynamite, firing incomprehensible Romanian at us, and at one point dragging us from the table to see the buffalo she kept in a shed at the back of her house. Now, we had already had lunch that day and weren't particularly hungry, and as I have said, balmos is very filling. We soldiered on and indeed it was delicious – well, if you were a navvy who hadn't eaten for a fortnight. Then Maria told us it could also be a sweet dish, and Kingy, deciding the only way he could stack more grub was to think of it as pudding, said, 'Oh, I would love to try the sweet version.' She promptly tipped about half a pound of sugar on his dinner. Tee-hee, I thought, fight through that one, Geordie.

Mamaliga is a staple here. In restaurants you are generally offered chips, rice or mamaliga as a side dish, very often with a fried egg and grated cheese on top. I particularly like left-over mamaliga fried in slices with some melted cheese. You are also offered smetana on the side. This is sort of like a mixture of sour cream and crème fraîche, but with a unique flavour. It can be used like mayonnaise, as a swirl in soup or goulash or, our favourite, on dill blinis with smoked salmon. (I never managed to get the hang of pronouncing it until I was told to say 'Santana', as in the rock band, with a 'sme' in front of it.)

To conclude, Romania was a great surprise. We expected a dull post-communist country with little to recommend it. We got a colourful, cultured country full of warmth and hospitality. Romanians truly have heart and soul. If you get the chance, go. They have everything, from beaches on the Black Sea to the Carpathian Mountains, which could rival the Alps, to the towns and villages of Transylvania and Maramures, which are like something from Hansel and Gretel. It is a country full of surprises.

SI AND DAVE'S LANGOSI
The Savoury One

This is great Romanian street food (pronounced 'langosh') that can be found on most street corners in Bucharest. Served either sweet or savoury, it is really tasty food on the go.

Makes 18–24 pancakes, depending on the size of your pan

for the batter
185g plain flour
75g buckwheat flour
2 tspns salt
½ tspn baking powder
335ml milk
2 tspns melted butter
2 eggs
butter to cook

for the tomato sauce
500g tomatoes (tinned is fine)
5 cloves of garlic, peeled and
   chopped finely

1 medium onion, peeled and chopped finely
1 tspn paprika
1 tbs parsley, chopped
1 tspn thyme
1 tspn oregano, chopped
2 tbs olive oil
6 capers
½ tspn sugar

to serve
ewe's milk cheese or mozzarella
fresh basil

To make the batter, blend the flours, salt and baking powder in a bowl, mix in the eggs, then add the milk and the melted butter. If your mixture is a bit like wallpaper paste, add more milk, a little at a time, until you have perfect batter the consistency of gloopy cream. You can leave this to stand for a bit in the fridge while you make the sauce.

If you're using fresh tomatoes, peel them first by blanching them in boiling water until the skins split, then removing them from the water so as not to cook them further. Once the tomatoes have cooled, the skins should come off nice and easy. Cut in half, de-seed and chop quite finely. Then sweat off the garlic and onion, add all the other ingredients, season, and simmer for about 10 minutes.

Now, with your lovely batter, make the pancakes. Heat a non-stick frying pan and lightly oil it before adding a ladleful of the pancake mixture, just enough to coat the bottom of the pan. Cook for 30–60 seconds until set on the bottom before flipping over to cook on the other side for another 30 seconds. Remove from the pan and put on a plate ready for loading. Then add the warm tomato sauce, cheese and basil leaves to one half of the pancake and fold the other half over the top. Dress with fresh tomatoes, basil leaves and a dusting of paprika and serve with a green salad.

SI AND DAVE'S LANGOSI
The Sweet One

Makes 14–18

for the batter
225g plain flour
2 eggs
pinch of salt
2 tbs caster sugar
675ml milk
2 tspns melted butter
½ tspn baking powder

for the raspberry coulis
250g raspberries
sugar to taste
cherry brandy to taste

for the hazelnut-cream filling
3 tbs butter
4 tbs cocoa powder
3 tbs caster sugar
½ tspn vanilla extract
225ml milk
4 egg yolks
150g hazelnuts, chopped
225ml whipping cream

to serve
icing sugar

Follow the method given on page 135 for your batter and set aside in the fridge. Mix up the ingredients for the coulis, then set that aside to meld, steep and generally improve whilst you get on with the filling.

In a bowl suspended over a pan of simmering water, melt the butter with the cocoa, stirring to mix, then take the bowl off the pan to cool.

In a separate bowl, cream together the sugar and egg yolks with an electric whisk till you get a fluffy and lightish colour on your yolks. Heat up the milk and add to the warmish chocolate mixture. Now add your sugar and egg mixture to the hot chocolate mixture in the first bowl, put it back over the pan of gently simmering water and stir for 12–15 minutes, taking great care not to heat it too quickly or it will turn to scrambled eggs. You want a beautiful, glossy sauce which is thick enough for there to be a bit of drag on your spoon when stirring.

Mix in the nuts and leave to cool. Finally, whip up the cream and add to the cooled mixture.

SPECK AND PORK SARMALE, With Mamaliga, Sour Cream and Ewe's Milk Cheese

The national dish of Romania is quite complicated but well worth it because it tastes great. It is brilliant winter fireside food but not ideal for cooking on a baking hot summer's day as we did.

Serves 8–10 in a very large dish!

for the sarmale
2 small heads of cabbage
800g jar of sauerkraut, drained (reserving about 225ml for the poaching liquid)

for the stuffing
750g pork shoulder, minced
250g speck
6 tbs olive oil
1 medium onion, peeled and finely chopped
8 cloves of garlic, peeled and finely chopped
2½ tbs rice
4 tbs hot water
1 slice of white bread
2 tbs dill, chopped
1 tbs thyme, chopped
tabasco to taste
2 tspns salt
1 tspn black pepper
2 tbs water

for the poaching liquid
1 litre water
225ml sauerkraut juice
10 black peppercorns
4 bay leaves
500g streaky bacon
500g tomatoes, sliced
a few dill fronds

for the mamaliga
175g polenta
1 litre water
1 tspn salt
a big knob of butter

to serve
grated ewe's cheese
sour cream
paprika

Take the big, outer green leaves off the cabbage and blanch for 2 minutes, then set aside. Core the cabbage, put in a big pot, hole-side down, and cook for 2 minutes with the lid on. Take out and, core-side up, strip away as many cabbage leaves as you can – the cooked roots at the base of each leaf should come away easily. Blanch the detached leaves and set aside after trimming off the thick stems. (This makes for easier rolling.) Shred the remaining heart, then mix with the drained sauerkraut.

Now for the stuffing. Sweat the onion and garlic in the olive oil for a few minutes, till translucent. Add the rice and stir briefly to coat with the oily onion and garlic, then add the hot water and simmer till it's absorbed – this takes about 9 minutes. While it's cooling, mix the minced pork with the speck and set aside. Then moisten the bread with water, squeeze dry, tear it into small pieces and blend with the meat. Add the rice mixture, the herbs and seasoning, and the 2 tablespoons of water. Mix well.

For the poaching liquid, mix the water with the sauerkraut juice, then add the peppercorns and the bay leaves. Then assemble the sarmale by putting a tablespoon of the stuffing in the centre of each of the inner cabbage leaves and rolling them up. Oil a big dish and first put a layer of the sauerkraut mixture, then a layer of bacon, then a layer of sarmale, and repeat till everything is used up, ending with a layer of sauerkraut. Then lay the fronds of dill on top and pour over the sauerkraut-juice mixture. Seal with the lovely set-aside outer cabbage leaves, dress with olive oil and simmer for about 1½ hours. Then peel back the green leaves, cover with sliced tomatoes and cook for another half an hour.

For the mamaliga, mix the polenta with the cold water and salt, add the butter and bring to the boil. Stir for about 10 minutes till the polenta comes together to form a ball-like mixture.

Serve a couple of the rolls with the juices and bacon bits, and a ball of the mamaliga with a coating of grated cheese. Have a big puddle of sour cream with a garnish of paprika on the side.

PRINCE CHARLES'S
CHICKEN-NOODLE SOUP
Made by Sara, Our Queen

This is food for the purist: the ultimate, organic, healthy chicken-noodle soup as cooked for HRH himself. It is the most wonderful, delicate dish and fit for a king (or a Kingy!). Our soup was served with home-baked bread and a potato salad – and, yes, Sara grew the potatoes herself. Aren't we lucky, and by heck don't we know it. Sara is one of the most wonderful women that we have ever met.

Serves 6–8

1 chicken, preferably free-range organic
2½ litres water
2 large onions, peeled and chopped finely
1 green pepper, sliced finely
large bunch of flat-leaf parsley, finely chopped
1 head of garlic

6 black peppercorns
1kg carrots, peeled and split lengthways
500g egg noodles

to garnish
a bit more flat-leaf parsley

If you were Sara, you would kill, pluck and draw your own chicken, then go to your well, fed by a pure mountain stream, pull the water and place it and the chicken in a pot with your home-grown onions, green pepper, parsley and garlic, all still covered with the dew from when you picked them some 5 minutes earlier. We just take one good free-range chicken and buy the best veg we can.

Add the peppercorns, then cover, bring to the boil and simmer gently over a two-hundred-year-old range for about 4 hours. Strain the broth, dispense with the lumpy bits, and set the chicken aside to make many other wonderful things. Add the carrots (Sara's could make Stevie Wonder see in the dark) and simmer for another 30 minutes. Then chuck in your egg noodles, made from your own eggs and flour, and simmer for 5 minutes.

Top with a sprinkling of finely chopped parsley and serve with pride.

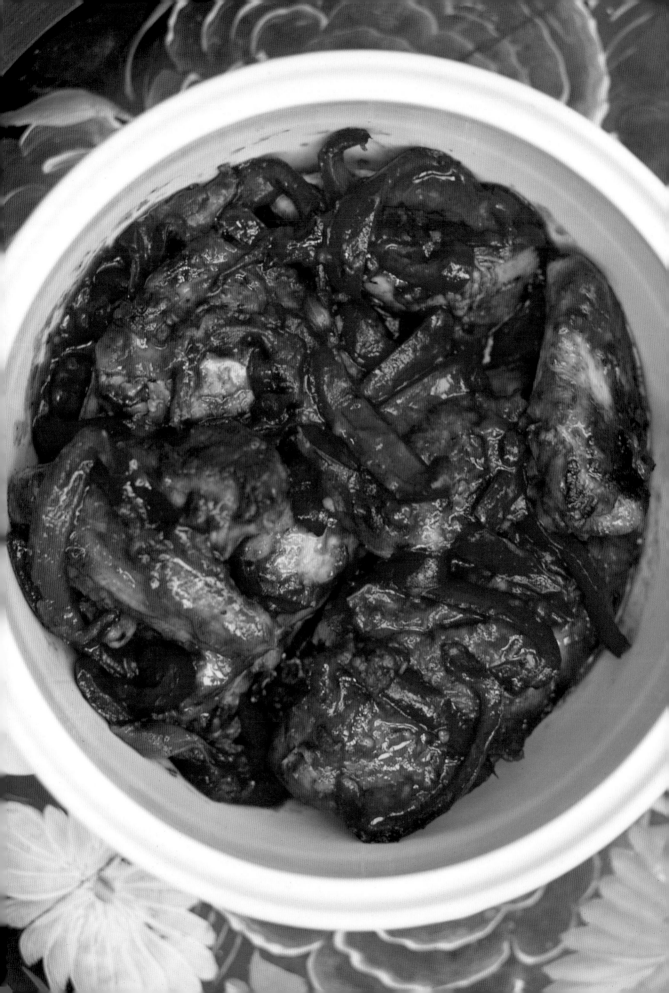

CHICKEN PAPRIKAS

Rich, red and ritzy, this is a favourite of ours. Three different paprikas add a smoky, sweet and spicy tang and it is a delight on the eyes and the mouth.

Serves 6–8

1 fat chicken

2 tbs olive oil

a large knob of butter

1 large onion, peeled and finely chopped

6 cloves garlic, peeled and finely chopped

1 tbs sweet paprika

1 tbs hot paprika

1 tbs smoked paprika

1 tbs flour

250ml chicken stock

a handful of flat-leaf parsley, chopped

2 red peppers, seeded and cut into 1cm strips

4 large, ripe tomatoes (or 6 tinned will do)

250ml sour cream or smetana

Joint the chicken (or get your butcher to do it). Rub the meat with salt, then brown in the oil and butter and set aside. In the same pan, sweat the onions and garlic for about 5 minutes. Add the paprika, then the flour, and stir till blended. Don't burn it! Add most of the stock and stir for 5 minutes to make the thick gravy base, then add the chicken pieces. Add the rest of the stock (and then some boiling water) if it looks a bit dry. Mix in half of the parsley and bring to the boil, then add the red pepper. Simmer for 10 minutes, add the tomatoes, then cook over a low heat for about an hour. When the chicken is cooked, add the sour cream and the remaining parsley. Adjust the seasoning and serve with the spaetzles.

LEMON AND BLACK-PEPPER SPAETZLES

Serves 6–8

140g flour

½ tspn baking powder

1 tspn salt

2 eggs

3 tbs water

2 tbs olive oil

a knob of butter

3 cloves of garlic, peeled and finely chopped

zest of 1 lemon

2 tbs lemon juice

1 tspn freshly ground black pepper

Blend the flour, baking powder and salt, work in the egg and add the water to make a thick batter. Force the batter through a large-bore perforated spoon into a pan of boiling water. It should form irregular-shaped, baby dumplings. After about 3 minutes, when the spaetzles have floated to the top, dry them on kitchen paper. Then, in a frying pan, sweat the garlic and lemon zest in the oil and butter, then fry the spaetzles until golden and add the lemon juice.

DILL BLINIS

These are worlds away from the little beer-mats available in the supermarket chiller cabinet. Top them with sour cream, fresh dill and either the best caviar you can afford or smoked salmon. Serve with the mititei and mustard.

Makes 20–25

60g buckwheat flour
170g plain flour
1 tspn salt
4g dried yeast
200ml crème fraîche

225ml whole milk
2 large eggs, separated
2 tbs fresh dill, finely chopped
butter to cook

Sift the flours and add the salt and yeast. In a saucepan, warm the crème fraîche and the milk to blood heat, whisk in the egg yolks and add to the flour mixture.

In a separate bowl, whisk the egg whites till peaky and fold into the dough. Add the dill and leave to rise in a warm place, covering the bowl with a tea towel. After an hour, the mixture will look bubbly and will have doubled in size.

Melt a knob of butter in a hot non-stick pan, place a tablespoon of blini mix in the pan then add a further ½ tsp to make the middle thicker. Turn when firm, cook till golden, cool on rack and enjoy.

THE PERFECT BLOODY MARY

Serves 8

vodka
tomato juice or V8
Worcestershire sauce
Tabasco
freshly ground black pepper
celery salt
lime juice
freshly grated horseradish
a splash of sherry if you fancy it

Assembly must vary according to your own tastes! Let's say celery, cucumber slices and fresh basil to garnish, but you could also use olives, dill pickles, peppers, baby corn, artichoke hearts, hearts of palm, king prawns, celery sticks, carrot sticks, lime wedges, water chestnuts or cherry tomatoes.

MITITEI OR 'LITTLE ONES'

These skinless sausages are Romania's fish and chips, served on every street corner with a dollop of Dijon-like mustard and cabbage salad. A spicy and moreish treat that's easy to make.

Serves 4

250g minced pork
250g minced beef
1 onion, peeled and finely chopped
3 cloves of garlic, crushed
$\frac{1}{2}$ tspn harissa paste
1 tspn sweet paprika
$\frac{1}{2}$ tspn smoked paprika
$\frac{1}{2}$ tspn cayenne pepper
$\frac{1}{2}$ tspn allspice (optional)
1 tspn thyme
1 tspn marjoram
$\frac{1}{2}$ tspn baking powder
1 tspn caraway seeds, soaked and ground
olive oil

Combine all the ingredients and knead for about 5 minutes to really meld the flavours. Work into small skinless sausage shapes, then fry or grill for 5–8 minutes. You can dribble stock on them as they cook – this will keep them juicy! Serve with mustard.

BLACK SEA

ARMENIA

TURKEY

CAPPADOCIA ● ● ● ● KAYSERI

VAN

KAHRAMANMARAS

MARDIN

IRAN

GAZIANTEP ● SANLIURFA

SYRIA

IRAQ

Turkey

SI: Turkey is a big country – a very big country, over 2,000km across. To the west it borders Greece and Bulgaria, to the east Syria, Iraq, Iran, Armenia and Georgia, and is topped and tailed by the Black Sea and the Mediterranean. Everyone knows about Antalya and the Brits in Bodrum, so we set out for the east and south-east, the parts that, what with the current troubles, a lot of people don't reach. Indeed, because of the situation between Turkey and the Kurds, the area around Van and Mount Ararat has only just been opened up.

We decided to start from the centre of the country, in Kayseri – a thriving commercial city with numerous street vendors flogging everything from ice cream to magic carpets – then drive to Cappadocia and the caves at Zelve, then follow the southern border east through Kahramanmaras, Gaziantep, Urfa, Mardin, Diyarbakir, Tatvan, Gevas and finally Van. This route would take in ancient Byzantine towns, some mentioned by monks as early as AD 100. Imagine shadowing the biblical figures, pilgrims and scholars who, since the death and ascension of the Messiah, have sought the way forward for all humanity... Well, in fact we were on a search for a kebab. Not just any kebab, oh no: we were on a quest for the kebab that defined the Turkish nation.

There was a slight flaw in our plan, however; the area had only recently been de-militarised due to the ongoing guerrilla war with the KKP, the Kurd nationalist organisation renowned for its skills in kidnap, ambush and, when called for, all-out assaults on the Turkish army. Having given the producers the heebie-jeebies about our planned route, they checked its safety with all the relevant organisations (always check with the Foreign Office before you go anywhere remotely dangerous). The response on the whole was very positive: all would be fine as long as we stuck to our route and the main roads, didn't travel at night and gave sensitive military areas a wide berth. We were also informed that most of the areas off the beaten track had more explosives buried than an Aerosmith gig, so were to be avoided.

DAVE: In Kayseri we visited a typical kebab shop, with a chicken doner turning in the corner that must have weighed fifty kilos. It had been made earlier that morning; by the evening it would be gone, or any remains given away. In England, the mysterious elephant-leg-like doner will stand there spinning for days on end, slowly shrinking as drunken customers on their way home from the pub succumb to its dubious charms. Occasionally, if it's lucky, it may get a night in the fridge. This Kayseri kebab was different. I had it with a fresh, parsley-loaded salad and the traditional flatbread. Si, on the other hand, was drawn to the barbecue of gothic proportions in another corner, where about a hundred chickens were slowly turning over a vast charcoal pit. About six men tended this beast, throwing bucketfuls of fresh spices over the golden meat. Kingy sat down to the best chicken ever.

From Kayseri we drove about 150km to Zelve, which has one of the most bizarre and beautiful landscapes in the world. Phallic rock formations, called fairy chimneys, are peppered with caves that were inhabited until the early 1950s. There, inspired by the Turks' love of pulses and fresh, colourful vegetables, and by the beds of vines lying in the scrub all around, we prepared a traditional vegetarian mezze. Vine leaves mean dolmas, those neat little parcels filled with lovely, sticky, aromatic rice: a great Virgo dish. On the rustic front, Kingy got his fire on and roasted some aubergines to perfection; the resulting purée was really smoky and tasty. We also made some traditional courgette and feta fritters (try saying that after a drink or two) and tangy houmus with yoghurt. Add to this kisir – the salad made with herbs, bulgar wheat and a spicy tomato dressing – some olives and good Turkish bread and we had quite a feast. We asked some local market traders to sample it and it went down a treat, with carry-outs requested by all.

Next we headed south to Gaziantep, close to the Syrian border. In some ways it is the gastronomic capital of Turkey, with an annual food fair, and you really begin to feel the Arabic influence here, like the real adventure is starting. It is also the pistachio capital of Turkey. When you buy a bag of pistachio nuts, you will notice that they are split open. This is not the way they come. Each nut has to be split, one by one, by someone with a small hammer. This thankless task is done by whole families, and mostly by the children. We visited a neighbourhood where families sit around tables, day in, day out, cracking nuts for hours on end. The problem is that the children are kept at home to do this rather than being allowed to go to school. The children we met were well cared for and seemed happy to be working in a family unit, with the love that comes with this, but it was a work-to-survive situation, and not ideal.

The finest pistachio nuts are used in the making of Gaziantep's other great product: baklava. Imam Cagdash's pastry room was possibly the worst environment that I have ever been in. The windows were covered with polystyrene tiles to keep the heat and humidity inside, and the flour was thick in the air, filling your eyes and lungs. About a dozen men work like demons in this hellish environment to create the finest pastry in the world. It is rolled by hand until it looks like sheets of silk, then a layer is placed on a tray, brushed with melted butter and another layer added. Ordinary baklava has up to fifteen layers; Imam Cagdash's has forty – the ultimate. The pastry is then baked in a wood oven before the 'syruping'. Imam's father is the only one allowed to do this. He pours the boiling syrup onto the baklava and it starts to 'dance like an Ismir girl'. (Note to self: must meet an Ismir girl!) Downstairs in the restaurant we taste the baklava. It is, quite simply, amazing.

We had heard that there are two places in the world that produce the best ice cream: Rome and Maras in Turkey. The beauty of doing this show is that when we hear something like this, we do a Norman Tebbit and get on our bikes and go. And when we reached Maras, we realised the whole town is devoted to ice cream. Now, Turkish ice cream is ace but it's not ice cream as we know it. It's called dondurma, can be flavoured with rose petals or orchid root, and it contains mastika, so it's chewy – indeed, you can cut it with a knife or make a rope with it and tow a car. The ice cream men are wacky, doing tricks with it, juggling with it, even making doners out of it and serving it on a spit! You kind of panic when you first put it in your mouth – you think it's stuck there for ever – but then, as it warms up, it dances down your throat.

Now, I have always wanted to build a doner; indeed I have often wondered, like other people, what on earth is in a doner. It's one of life's great mysteries, like why fat women wear leggings. When we reached Mardin, we visited a master kebab-maker to watch and learn. The next challenge was obviously to see whether two northern blokes could sell kebabs to the Turks. A couple of days before, we had met a wonderful family who took us into their home and to their hearts. After our lesson from the kebab-man, we arrived at their house and started to build our own doner while the women watched suspiciously.

'The last leg of our journey was up to the town of Van, a long way away from Mardin, on some pretty hard roads. The word "hairy" kept coming to mind – and I don't mean a couple of cuddly, fun-loving, foodie bikers.'

Then the men arrived home from work and the party started. As the meat cooked to perfection, we sliced off piece after piece with a knife the size of a broadsword. It went down a storm. As at every barbecue, every man present reckoned he was Gordon Ramsay, so eventually we stood back and let the fellers carve. It was a great night, watching from their terrace as the sun went down over the Mesopotamian plain and the lights started to sparkle over Syria. What a privilege.

It wasn't all fine dining and nifty panoramas, though. The history of the place keeps coming back to you, and sometimes it gets personal. While we were up on that rooftop terrace in Mardin, building our monster kebab, with that great view across the whole plain, our director Dave Rea suddenly realised that he was looking out at a piece of his own family history. His old dad had fought in World War I on those very same plains. And we're still fighting there now, almost one hundred years later, and still for no good reason.

The last leg of our journey was up to the town of Van, a long way away from Mardin, on some pretty hard roads. The word 'hairy' kept coming to mind – and I don't mean a couple of cuddly, fun-loving, foodie bikers – what with the unpredictable surfaces and the frenzy of trucks and petrol tankers hurtling out of Iraq straight at us, not to mention the armoured convoys of Kurd-busters. But the last miles of the drive are on lovely mountainous roads alongside Lake Van, a vast salt-water lake, very blue and calm, and apparently six times the size of Lake Geneva. And it's got its own Nessie, too . . .

We had heard about the Lake Van Monster, and with Van's exotic history and the lake being in the middle of former Kurdistan, we thought it was worth a look. After the mega-long drive we ended up in the grand office of the Mayor of Gevas, Nazmi Sezer. Filled with flags and a huge desk, it really was quite imposing – until we noticed that Mr Sezer was surrounded by plastic dinosaurs. He told us the tale of the monster, then picked one up and gave it a tweak. Squeak, squeak, it went. We tried so hard to keep straight faces. He has erected one statue of the monster in the town and another is planned. Kingy sucked all this in and later, when we met a man who claimed he had been attacked by the monster, he was convinced. So we spent days sitting by the lake waiting. Things only livened up when we managed to get some of the local hallucinogenic honey.

This hallucinogenic honey, or 'mad honey' as the locals call it, is not another tall tale. The bees get the pollen from azaleas, rhododendrons and other slightly toxic plants and those toxins stay in the honey. Indeed in Roman times the Emperor Pompeii's advance was halted by it when locals left honeycombs out for the soldiers to eat, then attacked and killed them when they became incapacitated. In the eighteenth century the honey was exported to Europe and sold to innkeepers, becoming very popular as an additive to your pint of beer. Result: smiley faces. Well, we had to get a jar. (It's strange stuff and you have to be very careful, so don't try this one at home because too much will stop your heart.) We love bananas and honey, so sitting on the shores of Lake Van we dipped our 'nanas into the pot and tucked in. All of a sudden we felt slightly euphoric and then we began to giggle. After a while we were like a pair of psychedelic Winnie the Poohs. I think I saw the monster that afternoon...

Van definitely has a slightly shady side. It's awash with smugglers from Iran and there's a thriving black-market economy, run by some pretty bloodthirsty types. You can get anything you want there. For example, it's easy to buy a petrol tanker to drive off in – though getting one without petrol in it costs extra. The trick is to start whistling nonchalantly when you stray into the path of smugglers. Stay away from KKP Kurdish separatists and the Turkish army too. And don't mention heroin, weapons or money-laundering. Our guide told us how to look out for the money-laundering shops; they look like travel agencies, empty but for three brochures yellowing in the window. Better keep whistling...

Before we left Van, we stopped in the old town for one of Yusef's famous breakfasts. There is a strong Kurdish presence in the town as the villages around it were moved in to try to stop people sheltering the KKP – and of course the food came with them. Yusef's breakfast is a mezze of about fifteen different dishes and is a legend. Only topped by the eccentricities of Yusef himself, who appears during your meal to scream riddles at you. If you get the answers right you get a present. What a great way to wake up!

BIKE BITS

Right at the start of our journey, on the outskirts of Kayseri, we were stopped by the police and fined for speeding. When I asked to see the evidence of this on a radar gun, the policeman laughed, unclipped his gun holster, handed me a piece of paper with a 90 Turkish Lira fine and told me in no uncertain terms to pay at the local police station. I nipped my cheeks, smiled and scarpered. Be prepared when entering or leaving any major town or city in Turkey for there to be police checkpoints to nab local and foreign road users alike. Try not to give them any excuse to stop you – not, I hasten to add, that they need one. Our advice is to remain calm and polite whatever the provocation, take your fine and walk away.

Another note of caution: the highways around major cities tend to be covered in diesel and the wearing course of the tarmac is often worn out. These road conditions, coupled with heavy traffic and unobservant, petulant drivers, do not make for stress-free motorcycling, so take it really easy and you'll reach your destination without bits of you missing.

By contrast, the open road heading east is a real treat: sweeping bends, majestic plains and biblical landscapes make for fulfilling biking. However, as you get nearer the Iraq border there are huge numbers of oil tankers delivering fuel and oil to northern Iraq (talk about coals to Newcastle) and the roads are under great pressure from the heat and volume of this heavy traffic. Something to watch out for particularly is deeply rutted tarmac. It's bloody dangerous, but if it takes you by surprise the best way to get through it, in our experience, is to power on and hold on.

The further east we travelled, the more frequent army roadblocks became. It goes something like this:

'Papers, please! Where are you from?'

'England.'

'Where are you going?'

'That's a very big gun.'

'Yes it is. Where are you going?'

'Bloody hell, that's a tank.'

'Yes sir, that's a tank. Now, where are you going?'

'England.'

'What?'

'Sorry, I mean Van.'

'Why?'

'To eat kebabs.'

'Do they have good kebabs in Van?'

'Yeah, we think so. And they have a monster as well, you know.'

'What?'

'A monster, the Lake Van Monster. I'm surprised you haven't heard of it!'

'No, I haven't, sir.'

'Excuse me, I don't mean to be rude, but would you mind pointing that gun at the floor? It's making me sweat a bit.'

'Oh, really? Why?'

'Well, it's a gun and I haven't had one pointed at me before and very soon I'll be making a mess in me leathers.'

'Oh. Sorry.'

'It's OK.'

'Nice bikes. Can you pull a wheelie on that?'

'No, erm, I haven't thought about it really.'

'Shame, that would be good to see.'

'Yes. Thank you.'

'Is your friend going the same way as you?'

'Yes, he is.'

'You may go. Let me know about the kebabs in Van on your way back. I'm stationed here for six months. We'll see each other again.'

'Will do. Bye!'

Now you must understand that the soldier's English was as patchy as my Turkish. Plus Dave had pulled up behind me on the bike with all the cameras on it, and, Dave being Dave, had kept them running throughout this dialogue. I had hoped that the soldiers wouldn't notice them if I kept chatting about monsters and kebabs. Dave smiled a lot and said thank you in Turkish and it worked – through the roadblock we tootled.

You know how bikers approach with caution people driving Volvos and white vans? Well, in Turkey you watch out for tourist buses from Tehran. The drivers are completely bonkers, wired on coffee and other substances, and drive like Satan with his arse on fire – very bad and very scary. They will appear from nowhere in your mirrors, six inches from your back wheel, with their deep, loud horns trying to force your kidneys out of your ears. Best advice is to get out of the way; they really are nuts.

If you're camping, the facilities get poorer the further away from the tourist traps you get, so go prepared for days of independent living. We would strongly recommend you treat yourself and stay in one of the numerous and historic caravanserai, places of refuge for the traveller and most of them hundreds of years old. They are comfortable, clean and worth a visit. While you're there, ask for a nargile (the traditional hubble-bubble pipe) with your coffee. They're lovely!

A good rule of thumb when stopping to eat is: the more trucks outside the better. The standard of road-food is good, primarily because the Turks just will not tolerate bad food, and you're guaranteed great company too. The men sit with each other, drinking tea and talking about things that men talk about. You'll be invited to join in, so please take the opportunity. It's polite to accept and some of the best information we found came from meetings like this. Don't worry about the language barrier: the Turks are very socially inclusive. No one cares if you can't speak Turkish, and it's a right laugh trying to make yourself understood.

In conclusion, we loved riding in Turkey. Just remember that it looks scarier than it actually is: once you're in the flow of traffic you become the master of your own destiny. The people are great too, if a bit in your face at times. The scenery is spectacular and of course there's the sheer quantity and variety of kebabs – oh, Utopia!

FOOD BITS

DAVE: Some people say there are three great cuisines in the world: Chinese, French and Turkish. I think this is a gross generalisation, but Turkey is certainly up there with the best of them: the Ottoman cuisine, with its particular approach to building flavour, is truly remarkable. When Mehmet II conquered Constantinople in 1453, the city became the centre of the Ottoman Empire and its culinary activities. Mehmet held great feasts at the Topkapi Palace, filling his kitchens with hundreds of specialist chefs. The *boreki* made tasty little pastries; the *kofteki* specialised in meatballs; and, high in status, the *baklavaki* were the highly skilled makers of baklava. The chefs competed to devise the best new recipes, creating the celebrated *saray*, or palace cuisine. We think we're foodies; we have nothing on the Ottomans.

The empire reached its zenith during the reign of Suleyman the Magnificent, who, amongst other small achievements, added a kitchen with six domes to the Topkapi Palace and increased the number of chefs to a thousand. European chefs visited, bringing their expertise and new ingredients with them (the Spanish and Portuguese brought tomatoes, potatoes, maize and chilli peppers, for example), and then in turn took Turkish influences home with them. In the seventeenth century a team of French chefs arrived... Well, egos kicked in when they began to get scales and ledgers out to write down the recipes. The Turkish chefs laughed at what they saw as amateurish accessories – couldn't they just taste the food? And with this the French were sent packing. I think maybe Kingy's cooking style is a bit Ottoman: constant tasting and chucking bits of this and that in until he gets what he wants. Me, I like a plan. *Vive la France*! The sultan's kitchen is now open to the public, so a pilgrimage is necessary – the Canterbury Cathedral of foodie nuts!

Suleyman the Magnificent was also the first to bring the harem to the palace. With the arrival of the girls such dishes as the syrupy dessert kiz memesi (young girls' breasts) and kadin gobegi (ladies' navels) were created. I think the sultan would have been a biker if he was around today. Can you imagine how brilliant it was to be him? You come home after a run out, set a thousand chefs to work sorting you out a kebab, get down the harem to ask a couple of chicks out, all rounded off with a plate of ladies' navels... Mind, I bet there were times when he came home and thought, oh no, not more blooming belly dancers. All I fancy is a night in watching the telly with a pasty and chips.

As the empire expanded so did the cuisine, as the Turks adopted the best of the local foods. In turn they influenced the Greek, Romanian, Hungarian, Russian and north African cuisines, which is why we find variations of kebab, kofte, dolmas, baklava and Turkish coffee in these countries. It's with delight I remember the dolmas stuffed with minced chicken and dill in Romania, even thought the Turks also gave them their favourite tripe soup.

KISIR SALAD

Get this right and it's a really satisfying dish to produce.

Serves 6 healthy appetites

115g bulgar wheat soaked in boiling water
  for about 1 hour

the white bits of 4–5 spring onions,
  chopped finely

4 cloves of garlic, peeled and
  chopped finely

1 green chilli, de-seeded and chopped finely

2 tspns chilli flakes

2 tbs tomato paste or Turkish salça

2 tbs red pepper paste

2 tbs olive oil

2 tbs flat-leaf parsley, chopped

2 tbs fresh mint, chopped

1 romaine lettuce

Drain the wheat, wrap it in a tea towel and squeeze it dry. Mix everything up except the lettuce, and get stuck in, kneeding it with your hands. Serve it on a bed of lettuce leaves. The bright red salad and the leaves look ace. It also tastes mega with the dolmasi.

HOUMUS

This is loads better than the stuff in tubs. A tip we picked up in Turkey is to add yoghurt to the mixture which tastes lovely.

Serves 6

2 tins of chickpeas, or 170g dried ones
  soaked overnight

4–6 tbs olive oil

juice of 1 lemon

4–5 cloves garlic, peeled and crushed

1 tbs tahini

1 tspn cumin powder

½ tbs yoghurt

to serve

olive oil

chilli flakes

pine nuts

flat-leaf parsley, chopped

Cook the chickpeas in a liberal quantity of boiling water until soft – or open the cans and drain! Grind them to a paste with a masher or blender, add the olive oil, lemon juice, garlic, tahini, cumin and yoghurt, and season to taste. Mix the chilli flakes with the oil and drizzle artistically on the houmus. Scatter a few pine nuts and the parsley on top, and bingo: instant Turkish wedding!

YALANCI YAPRAK DOLMASI
or Veggie Dolmas

Dolmas are stuffed vine leaves found throughout the Mediterranean and the Middle East and they are a toothsome delight. You can also make them with minced lamb, pine nuts and rice but our veggie ones are banging.

Serves 6

2 packs of preserved vine leaves, or as many as you want to make (or pick them fresh and blanch them!)
225g short-grain or pudding rice
2 onions, peeled and finely chopped
3 cloves garlic, peeled and crushed
2 tbs olive oil
a knob of butter
1 tbs sugar
2 tbs currants

2 tbs pine nuts
½ tspn allspice
½ tspn cinnamon
¼ tspn ground cloves
bunch of flat-leaf parsley, chopped
bunch of mint, chopped
bunch of dill, chopped
285ml water
2 tbs olive oil
2 tbs lemon juice

First plunge your vine leaves in boiling water and leave to steep for 20 minutes (this is very important if you are using preserved leaves as it will remove the bitterness of the preservatives). While this is going on, soak the rice in warm water for 10 minutes. Sweat the onions and garlic in the oil and butter, and when transparent add the sugar, currants and pine nuts and cook for a couple of minutes. Stir in the spices and rice, and season to taste. Add the water till it just covers the mixture, and bring to the boil. Simmer for about 12 minutes or until the liquid is absorbed and the rice is almost cooked, but still has some bite. Mix in the fresh herbs and leave them to wilt for about 5 minutes; this will also give the filling time to cool so you don't burn your digits.

Take the leaves out of their steeping water, discarding any that are holey or ripped, and rinse a couple of times with cold water to get rid of any salt. Lay a leaf out in front of you, veiny side up. Put about a dessertspoon of filling just above the stem, then fold the stem over the filling, wrap the two side leaves over and roll the dolma up. Repeat till you have about 60 – it's fiddly at first but by number 20 you will have the hang of it. Place a layer of vine leaves on the bottom of a large saucepan, then pack the dolmasi in a snug, even layer, cover with another layer of leaves and repeat till they are all put to bed. Cover with the remaining leaves and place a plate on top with a weight on it so that they don't unroll (or use the special terracotta plate with holes in that the Turks use).

With the plate still in place, add the 285ml of water, the olive oil and lemon juice, bring the water up to the boil and simmer for 1 hour. Leave to cool in the pan, then carefully unpack them, pile them on a plate with lemon to garnish and enjoy.

KABAK MÜCVERI
or Courgette and Feta Fritters

A few of these would make a great vegetarian main course with a salad. They are easy to make and brilliant to eat.

Makes 18 fritters

680g courgettes
the white bits of a bunch of spring onions, chopped finely
2 tbs fresh dill, chopped
2 tbs flat-leaf parsley, chopped
3 eggs, beaten
1 tspn paprika
225g feta cheese
150g plain flour
groundnut oil for frying

Grate the courgettes (watch your fingers!), apply a few big pinches of salt and let them drain for 20 minutes. Next, place in a clean tea towel and squeeze out the water. You will be left with a courgette ball. Mix with the onions, dill, parsley, eggs and paprika, and season with salt and pepper. Work in the feta cheese and flour; you should be left with a mixture the consistency of porridge.

Spoon out a tablespoon of the mixture into the hot oil and fry until golden. Garnish with slices of lemon.

HÜNKAR BEGENDI or Sultan's Delight, With Turkeyshire Pudding and Piyaz Pilaf

Hünkar begendi, a delicious Ottoman feast of lamb and aubergine, was a favourite at the Topkapi Palace, the centre of Turkish culinary magic. We have given this an original twist by serving it with a spicy Yorkshire pudding. The three components work really well together: the crispy, aromatic Turkeyshire pudding with the rich lamb stew and the heavenly, creamy, smoky aubergine.

SULTAN'S DELIGHT

Serves 8

the lamb

55g butter

3 tbs olive oil

1.4kg lamb shoulder or leg, trimmed and cut into 2cm cubes

1 onion, peeled and chopped finely

5 cloves of garlic, peeled and chopped finely

2 tbs tomato paste

½ tspn dried thyme

1 tspn dried oregano

¼ tspn cloves

½ tspn allspice

1 tspn ground cumin

565ml lamb stock

the begendi, or aubergine sauce

4 large aubergines

225ml milk

2 tbs double cream

55g butter

1 tbs plain flour

115g kasseri cheese, grated (cheddar will do)

1 tspn chilli flakes

to garnish

flat-leaf parsley

Melt the butter and oil in a heavy pan and brown the lamb for about 5 minutes, stirring frequently. Add the onion and garlic and sweat down for a couple of minutes. Add the tomato paste, herbs, spices and stock, and season. Bring to the boil and simmer with the lid on for 40 minutes, then take the lid off for a further 20 minutes, till the stew is thick and the meat tender.

Meanwhile, bake the aubergines over charcoal, gas flame or in the oven, as described above. Peel and pulp them, and then (if you're feeling vindictive) pass them through a sieve. In a saucepan, warm the milk and cream, while in another pan melt the butter and work in the flour. Add the milk-cream mixture to the second pan to make a white sauce. When the mixture begins to thicken, add the aubergine purée, cheese and chilli flakes, and season to taste. Stir over a low heat for about 5 minutes to cook out the flour.

TURKEYSHIRE PUDDING

This is a gorgeous fusion of Barnsley and Bodrum, and is served on the lamb with its gravy on the top.

Serves 8

4 heaped tbs plain flour
1 tspn salt
1 tspn cumin seeds
1 tspn ground cumin
½ tspn allspice
2 eggs
285ml milk
groundnut oil

Mix the flour, salt, cumin seeds, ground cumin and allspice. Make a well in the middle and crack in the eggs. Think cement mixing as you work the eggs into the mixture. Whisk in the milk, then, when lumpless, set aside to rest for 30 minutes. (This is important to get the best pudding.) Meanwhile, put your oven on at 200°C and put a 5cm roasting dish with a splash of groundnut oil into it to heat up.

When your mixture is rested and your oil is smoking, pour in the mixture so that it's about 1cm deep (we want sort of cocktail Turkeyshire puddings), then bake for about 20 minutes until risen like Lazarus on speed.

To serve, place a dollop of each of the elements of the dish on a large plate with the Turkeyshire pudding and the rice and garnish with the parsley. Bloody gorgeous.

PIYAZ PILAF

4 tbs butter
300g long-grain rice
600ml chicken stock

Melt the butter and stir in the rice for a couple of minutes. Pour in the stock and season, bring to the boil, cover and simmer for about 15 minutes, or until all the stock has been absorbed and the rice is cooked. Serve in a bowl on the side of the hünkar begendi.

PATLICAN EZMESI

or Aubergine Purée, With Olive Oil and Lemon Juice

Like dolmas, a version of this aubergine purée can be found throughout the Mediterranean and the Middle East. Grilling the aubergine enhances the flavour and gives it a wonderfully seductive aroma.

Serves 6

3 large aubergines
2 tbs lemon juice
3 cloves garlic, peeled and chopped finely
2 tbs olive oil
1 tbs yoghurt

to garnish
bunch of flat-leaf parsley
1 red onion, peeled and sliced into rings

Roast the aubergines, preferably over a charcoal fire, as we want a nice smoky taste. If you can't do this, then hold them over a gas flame until black all over and the insides are very squashy (or you could just roast them in the oven at 240°C for about 45 minutes). Scoop out the flesh and mix with the lemon juice, garlic, olive oil and yoghurt. Season to taste, and garnish with the red onion rings and parsley.

THE MONSTER DONER KEBAB

A gastronomic mystery laid bare ... *do* try this at home!

Serves 50!

15kg leg of lamb, trimmed
3kg sheep's tail fat

for the marinade
125ml milk
125ml olive oil
2 tbs allspice
1 tbs ground cloves

6 eggs
1 tbs thyme
2 tbs ground cumin
1 tbs chilli flakes
1 tbs garlic flakes
200g dry onions

Trim the fat and other bits off the lamb and set aside. Then start to butterfly the lean meat into very thin slices, and hammer them even thinner. This is very skilful and takes a long time. Mince the trimmings (you'll end up with about 3 kilos). Make the marinade by mixing all the ingredients, and leave the meat and the mince to marinate in it overnight.

Next day, cut the sheep's tail fat into slices and start to build your monster. First, put a slice of fat on the base of the kebab machine and add three leaves of meat. Then form a thin burger with some of the mince, poke a little hole in the middle and thread it onto the kebab. Repeat, trying to build the shape out as you go, packing the mince around the central skewer and constantly trimming and adjusting. When the beast is built, stand back, admire and have a cup of tea – you've earned it.

Leave the doner for an hour or so to settle. The weight of the kebab causes it to compress so that you get the typical doner texture, but not the horrid processed feel you can get when it's been made of salvaged and reconstituted stuff.

Now, light the machine and let the doner warm through gently for an hour. Then, turn the heat up. The sheep's tail fat will melt, making the lean meat lovely and juicy. As it becomes crispy, slice off thin pieces with the biggest, sharpest knife you can find.

ACI KIRMIZI BIBER SALÇASI
or Chilli Sauce

This is hot hot hot, so please wear gloves or watch where your hands go after they've touched the chillies…

Makes about 750ml

455g chilli peppers
455g red bell peppers
about 1½ litres water
1 tspn sugar
2 tbs white-wine vinegar
2 tbs olive oil

Boil the peppers up in the water for about 15 minutes, then leave to cool. Peel the peppers and purée. Put in a pan with the sugar, and add salt to taste. Simmer uncovered for about 30 minutes to concentrate the sauce. Add the vinegar and the oil, and pour into sterilised jars.

IÇ PILAVI

or Chicken Liver and Almond Pilaf

This almond pilaf is a happy marriage of delicate chicken livers with nuts and spices, topped with fresh dill, saffron and parsley. It's the pilaf that out-risottos risotto.

Serves 6

2 tbs butter
4 cloves of garlic, peeled and chopped finely
1 medium onion, peeled and chopped finely
2 tbs pine nuts
2 tbs almonds, chopped roughly
1 tbs currants
¼ tspn allspice
1 tspn dried basil

455g chicken livers, trimmed of all stringy bits and chopped finely
bunch of flat-leaf parsley, chopped finely
bunch of dill, chopped finely
340g long-grain rice
850ml chicken stock

to garnish
saffron and flat-leaf parsley

In a large saucepan, melt the butter and sweat down the garlic and onion. Stir in the nuts and currants and cook for 2 minutes. Add the allspice, basil and the chicken livers, brown lightly (about 7 minutes on a high heat), season and chuck in the fresh herbs. Leave to wilt for 30 seconds, then remove the mixture from the pan and set aside. Toss the rice in the buttery residue in the pan for 1–2 minutes, pour over the stock and bring to the boil. Simmer gently for a few minutes till the stock starts to get absorbed, then carefully fold in the liver mixture. Turn off the heat, seal the pan lid on with a folded tea towel and leave to stand for 15 minutes. Fluff up and serve with the saffron and parsley garnish.

ÇOBAN SALATASI
or Shepherd's Salad

Sumac is a common spice in Arabic cooking. It is a beautiful deep-red colour and has a deliciously tart, citrus flavour. You can find it in specialist shops or online.

Serves 6

1 small cucumber, chopped
1 red onion, peeled, halved and sliced
2 big tomatoes
1 chilli, de-seeded and finely sliced
4 cloves garlic, peeled and chopped finely
a big bunch of flat-leaf parsley, chopped
1 tbs fresh dill, chopped
1 tbs fresh mint, chopped
2 tbs olive oil

2 tbs lemon juice
2 tspns sumac
2 pieces toasted pitta bread, chopped into small bits
1 romaine lettuce
assorted olives

to dress
pomegranate molasses

First, blanch the tomatoes in boiling water, leave to cool, then skin, de-seed and chop them. Combine the first 11 ingredients and leave to steep for 30 minutes so that the flavours marry together. Place the pitta bits and the olives on a bed of lettuce, pour over the salad mixture and dress with the pomegranate molasses.

AZURE
or Noah's Pud

This is what Noah (or probably Mrs Noah) is supposed to have cooked with what was left in the Ark's larder when it beached on Mount Ararat. It is a great leftover if you make too much.

225g barley
55g haricot beans
55g chickpeas
55g lima beans (or, if you can't find,
  add another 55g of chickpeas)
1.1 litres milk
565ml water
55g pudding rice
115g dried apricots
115g sultanas
55g currants
zest of 1 lemon
2 tspns cinnamon
1 tspn allspice

455g sugar
2 tbs cornflour mixed with 1 tbs milk
55ml rosewater

for the topping
55g dried figs
55g dried apricots
55g walnuts
1 tbs pinenuts
55g pistachio nuts
1 tbs currants

to serve
double cream

Soak the barley and any other dried pulses overnight in a liberal quantity of water. Strain, then simmer in the milk and water until they are tender. Add any canned pulses, the rice, apricots, sultanas and currants, and cook for 5 minutes. Then add the lemon zest, cinnamon and allspice and cook for another 10 minutes. Next, add the sugar bit by bit. When it begins to thicken, add the slaked cornflour.

Pour in the rosewater and simmer for another few minutes until the mixture has thickened up nicely. Tip into a large serving bowl and leave to cool. Scatter the nutty, fruity topping over it and serve with some double cream for extra indulgence.

Vietnam

HÒA XÃ HỘI CHỦ NGHĨA
VIỆT NAM

NĂM MƯỜI
NGHÌN ĐỒNG

50.000

DAVE : Vietnam is a thin ribbon of a country with two big blobs of land on either end. The Vietnamese liken it to the yokes with rice pails that the women carry in the streets, a simile that fits even better because rice production is concentrated in the north and south. Another popular image is of the country as a house with open windows on each of its four walls through which the four winds blow, rearranging the furniture before blowing out the other side. The long borders have always made Vietnam open to foreign influences, and most facets of Vietnamese life can be traced to the different invaders over the years, including China, India and France. This blend has created a delicious cuisine that is uniquely Vietnamese and begs to be explored.

What a trip. You land in Ho Chi Minh City (Saigon) and, bang, it's immediate sensory bombardment as you get caught up in the throng of people and motorbikes. They say that the brain of Vietnam is Hanoi, the heart imperial Hue and the stomach Ho Chi Minh. (And our first trip was down the Mekong Delta, the river that runs from near Ho Chi Minh to the sea, which I suppose in the anatomical drawing of Vietnam makes it the alimentary canal...)

Ho Chi Minh is a radical place and one thing that cannot be ignored is what we would regard as quite strange food. But to the Vietnamese there is nothing weird about food that will sustain the body: it's either wholesome or it's not. A large part of the Vietnamese diet is based on what is available, and some of that is quite, well, hardcore. Our first whiff of this was when a lady approached us in the street and offered us a couple of pulsating net bags. One was full of a selection of poisonous snakes, and in the other was a hooded cobra, which she wanted to sell to me for 200,000 dong – about £6. I asked her what on earth I would do with a deadly poisonous snake. Well, thoughts of tipping him into Kingy's leathers and blagging his wages had come to mind, but she snapped back: 'Hotpot!' By 'eck, never has a Lancashire staple taken on such exotica! I thought it would make an interesting cookery item, but the crew, doubting my snake-handling abilities, vetoed the project. However, a couple of days later in a local restaurant we ran into cobra hotpot again. It seemed like your everyday Vietnamese café until we looked up and saw the menu: scorpion, grasshopper, field rat, turtle dove, cobra, coconut worms, sparrows, deer and goat penises, minced bat, fieldmouse and frog's bladder…yum yum. We decided to give it a go – after all, whole villages survived for generations on this type of food.

We thought we would start with a couple of scorpions. Four crispy fried scorpions, minus sting, arrived cooked in chilli. They looked bloody awful. You eat them whole, like a soft-shelled crab, and they tasted a bit like pork crackling, but as we got past the heads their charm diminished. What next? Well, we left the field rat alone (we figured that we had a fair chance of getting a sewer rat in this city). The cobra: how did we want it? Like experts, we replied that a hotpot would be fine. It was like chomping an old dog chew – not recommended. The turtle doves, sparrows and bats were off, so we ordered the coconut worms, which arrived toasted with chilli. They really were quite nice, but then the waiter, now our new best mate, gave us a treat of half a dozen wriggling live ones in a drop of fish sauce. Neither of us could eat that.

Onward! Let's have a penis. The waiter said the deer penis was too big for two and that we should settle for a goat's; after all, it came complete with the testicles. This too came as a hotpot. (Imagine that down the pub: 'All right, love, I'll have the willy hotpot. Oh, and make sure you leave the bollocks on!') It came, and, well, Si tackled the, ahem, long bit whilst I tucked into the nuts. It tasted . . .

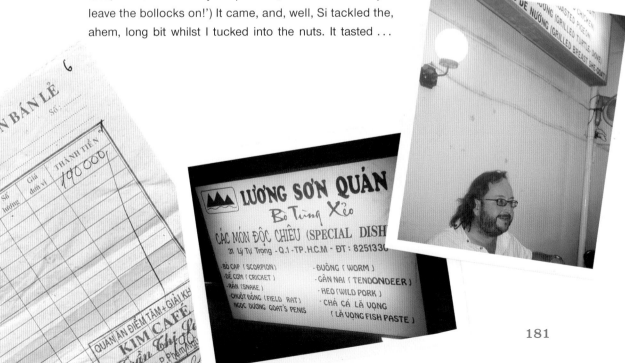

well, like a load of old balls. Not recommended. Enough was enough, so we asked for a little after-dinner drink. A bottle of 'snake wine' arrived, rice wine in which a cobra has been pickled. It is meant to be an aphrodisiac and tastes like rough whisky, but then your lips tingle and your face flushes and you start to have palpitations. Oo-er, let's have another. By this time your blood is rushing around your body. Time to stop. We paid our not-insubstantial bill, refused a complimentary frog's bladder and staggered back to the hotel. Well, yes, we did get a bowl of pho and some chips on the way back!

Next day we headed for the biggest market, Ben Thanh, which is more of a village within the city. As you approach, you pass countless street-traders selling some of the best food in Vietnam. There are stalls selling the ubiquitous pho, pork balls, and baguettes filled with fried egg and crispy pork – their version of a bacon and egg sandwich but fragrant with fish sauce, chilli and ram, which is like a cross between mint and coriander. Beautiful girls press sugarcane, mix it with lime and ice and serve it in plastic bags with straws poking out one corner, a truly refreshing drink. People sit making tiny rice-flour pancakes topped with dried shrimp and a sprinkling of beanshoots. These incredible morsels cost pennies and the stall-holders can make them as fast as you can eat them. It's a grazer's paradise.

As you enter the market, you see the vegetables first: water vegetables picked that morning from the Mekong Delta and root veggies from the farmers in the central highlands. The Vietnamese would never touch anything that is less than super-fresh. This goes for fish and meat too. The seafood is sold live and either killed and cooked in front of you, or taken straight home. It can be a bit strange at first, your bags of crabs and prawns kicking and scraping on the bus home.

There is a frequently repeated mantra in Vietnam that it is a country, not a war. Indeed it is, but the wars the country has experienced cannot be avoided. Forty kilometres outside Ho Chi Minh are the Cu Chi tunnels. These were built during the 1945–54 war against the French colonists, and became a major thorn in America's side during the war in the 1960s. The tunnels are now an impressive museum. Ingenious as ever, there is a unique tourist attraction: the firing range. Now, I know it's wrong, or at least politically incorrect, but I thought: go for it, just once in your life. So, you buy your bullets and choose your gun. It could be a Kalashnikov, an M60 machine gun, a Magnum or my weapon of choice, the massive machine gun off a Huey helicopter. It was an *Apocalypse Now* moment as we set off with our 'pieces', Kingy with his M60, me with my, err, big gun, and a couple of bandoliers of bullets. We reached the firing range in the jungle. Ooh Rambo, these beasts are scary – you twitch your finger and all hell breaks loose. It was great. This was until we remembered what these things are designed to do to other people. Nah, not right . . .

At the end of our journey, we had a final cultural and culinary hit in a Hanoi beer hall. Every night after work the locals go to these halls to drink pint after pint of 'fresh beer', a light pilsner lager that is brewed daily without preservatives, and is meant to be drunk immediately. It's the working man's refreshment and very palatable it is too. Si and I got stuck in, pint after pint went down, and the locals at the next tables became best pals. We started feeling peckish. The menu was in Vietnamese so, with a lot of pointing, we ordered a random selection of grub. A fish with Cantonese rice was spectacular. Then some grilled meat arrived with a side dish of rather skinny black pudding. 'Egh, this duck's tough,' said Si.

'Nah, it ain't duck, it's got four trotters. It must be a really scabby sucking-pig.'
'No! I know my pork – it's duck.'
'Well, have it your own way. What's the black pudding like?'
'Not very nice, Dave. It's not like Bury Market.'

I had got a piece stuck between my teeth and was digging away with a toothpick whilst Si tucked into the creature through a beery haze. Then Vikram, our director, held a piece of paper up out of shot. Si went very quiet. It read: D O G...

Oh no, we'd vowed we would never eat dog! 'Oh bugger,' I said, 'I've got a lump of Jack Russell stuck between me teeth, haven't I?'

All I can say is, eating dogs is bad and unnecessary. And they taste awful.

Our concluding moment in Vietnam came at the University of Literature in Hanoi. This is one of the oldest universities in the world, and a wonderful place of calm and learning. The roll of honour is on stone tablets mounted on the backs of stone turtles. Some of the graduates go back over a thousand years. There is a pagoda with a statue of Confucius, the great Chinese teacher. For over a thousand years, students have come to light incense and to pray for success in their exams. Confucius says: 'To learn without thinking is to labour in vain; to think without learning is desolation.' We say: 'Never trust a thin cook.'

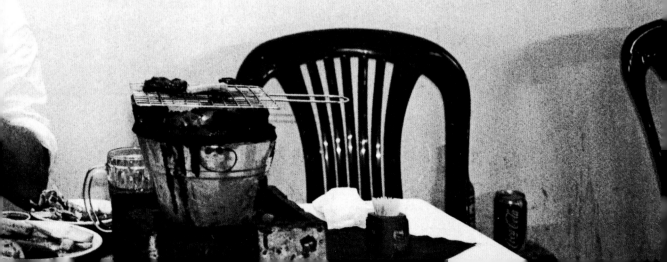

FOOD BITS

China ruled Vietnam for over a thousand years and brought Buddhism and rice cultivation. Indian flavours arrived via Cambodia, and Thailand and Laos contributed lemongrass, mint, chilli, basil and shrimp paste. Then, a while later, came the French, who taught the Vietnamese their whole cooking philosophy (and how to go 'pah' and curl your lip), and brought baguettes, beer and pâté. Now, apply all that to one of the most amazing culinary palettes and you have something really special. Those that say it's a cross between Chinese and Thai food are wrong; Vietnamese food is much subtler than both, and has a distinctive character all its own. They really are alchemists with food, delighting in ever-more-exciting combinations of flavour and texture.

The dish that you cannot ignore is pho (pronounced 'fer'). In the tenth century, the Mongol herdsmen brought its basic ingredient, beef. In the nineteenth century, the French introduced their method of making stock, and modern pho was born. Originally from the north, there isn't a corner of Vietnam now that doesn't sell it night and day. Some of the best is to be found on the streets, served out of mobile kitchens with all the accoutrements. As Si and I perched precariously on tiny stools – you know, the sort that toddlers get in playgroup – and the local folk cackled as the legs began to buckle, we started with large bowls of beef broth, made from shin bones and flavoured with star anise, ginger, cloves and cinnamon. This will have been simmering away for a day or so. A handful of cooked rice noodles are then thrown in to reheat, followed by sliced spring onions and raw beef. This is then handed to you and you do the rest yourself. You have a tray of spring onions, beanshoots, mint, basil, coriander and any other herbs of the day, some sliced chilli and slices of lime. You add what you want, then top the whole thing off with a seasoning of fish sauce. As you stir it all together, the herbs wilt and add flavour to the broth and the beanshoots give it crunch. Sometimes you can add some well-done brisket, so even the beef has two textures. It's sublime, and traditionally served for breakfast. Once you get used to it, it's a delicious and very healthy start to the day.

As you head north, the food changes. Hue is a truly magical place full of history, conflict, myth and legend, where you get a true sense of the heart, romance and the serenity of Vietnam. Hue is also the centre of the imperial cuisine, the equivalent of the Ottoman kitchens that we saw in Turkey. The Emperor Tu Duc of the mid-nineteenth century was a fussy eater. He demanded different food to what everyone else ate, every meal had to consist of fifty dishes, and he was not to be served the same menu twice in the same year. Thus the kitchens in the imperial palace had to show an enormous amount of ingenuity, refining and tarting up ordinary dishes before they were set before the Emporer. His chefs were said to be able to cook well over 2,000 menus, and the food was characterised by its beautiful decoration. We had a Hue banquet and it really was like a kind of overblown provincial dinner party of the 1970s. You know, a fish-mousse-with-cucumber-scales type of thing, although this one would

be complete with a carrot coral reef and a cucumber carved to look like a passing junk. When the pork pâté arrived in the shape of an elephant, complete with celery tusks, pea eyes and a lifelike handler sculpted from a radish, we longed for some plain old rice and pork.

We had to try another rare delicacy in this region, bird's-nest soup, which the Emperor Ming Mang claimed enhanced his sexual prowess and virility; indeed many restaurants that serve it are close to 'massage parlours'. If you order this in the UK, it is just a compressed scoop of noodles; true bird's-nest soup is a rare, expensive commodity. The nests are made from the saliva of the red-rumped swift, are only found high up in caves on certain islands, and are difficult and dangerous to collect. The main island is controlled by the government to stop poaching, but violent gangs have moved into other areas. The soup itself is delicious, similar to a very, very fine egg-noodle chicken broth. (One word of warning: when it was mentioned that we wanted to try it for a BBC programme we had to get government agreement first, as bird flu was rife in the area. *Bon appetit!*)

In Hoi An we were treated to coa lau, the Rolls-Royce of the noodle world. They are similar to Japanese egg noodles; indeed they can be traced back to the Japanese traders who settled here for many centuries. We visited a coa lau-maker who has been producing them for over a hundred years, and watched the process. First the rice is washed several times, with water drawn from a particular well (some coa-lau fanciers claim that they can tell if water from a different source has been used), then it is squeezed, husked, polished and ground. After the ground rice has dried, ash from the fire is added, which gives the noodles their distinctive yellow colour. The noodle dough is made from the dried rice and the ashes with water from the same well, then rolled out and cut by hand into thick strips. The traditional way of serving them is with pork cooked in fish sauce, fresh herbs, beansprouts and sliced onion. Banh da, a sort of super-sized, super-tasty prawn cracker, can also be crumbled in. With its balance of sweet and sharp, hot and bland, plus the bite of the meat, the sticky noodles, the thin sauce and the crispy cracker, it's a very Vietnamese combination of flavours and textures.

In Hanoi, we learnt more about Vietnamese cuisine from the celebrated French chef Didier Corlou. After a classical French training, he became enchanted with Asia, married a Vietnamese lady and settled in Hanoi, where he is head chef at the Metropole, with its amazing Spice Garden Restaurant. Didier is passionate about Vietnamese cooking and constantly pushes the creative boundaries, without ever losing sight of the street roots of the food. We met him in his kitchen, a lively, happy place with about 80 staff, and then adjourned to his office, where he told us his food philosophy. We couldn't get a word in edgeways, which was a major achievement. The food we tasted there was simply some of the best we have ever had. Some of the tastes I had never experienced before – not where you say, 'Ooh, it's a bit like…No, they were unique. The next night, he organised a fifteen-course taster menu for us. 'Don't worry: I will take you from south to north Vietnam in this menu.' 'Ooh, very nice,' we replied. The presentation was amazing: little titbits served on slabs of granite, tiny cups of soup that got progressively richer, seared foie gras with a light tamarind sauce. This was food as art.

Finally the coffee came, made from freshly ground Vietnamese beans. It tasted magic. (The strange orange powder sprinkled on top turned out to be wild bee pollen.) Vietnam is the second biggest coffee exporter in the world after Brazil. One of the more extreme varieties is civet, or weasel coffee, which is coffee that has been passed through a weasel's system. Apparently weasels will eat only the best coffee beans. As the beans pass through them, they mature and get more yummy. Some poor individual then collects the weasel droppings, washes them and extracts the partially digested coffee beans, which are then made into a brew. Despite all this, it is one of the nicest cups of coffee I have ever had. Sadly, a lot of the civet coffee is now fake. The Vietnamese have even developed a machine to simulate a weasel's internal workings to speed up production. Oh, what will they think of next…

'We had to try another rare delicacy in this region, bird's-nest soup, which the Emperor Ming Mang claimed enhanced his sexual prowess and virility; indeed many restaurants that serve it are close to "massage parlours".'

BIKE BITS

SI: As you know by now, there are no bad bikes: all are loved and cherished, no matter what they are. I'm glad you're on our wavelength because Vietnam is a case in point.

The bike culture of Vietnam is truly astounding. Ninety per cent of the population has some form of two-wheeled transport under 125cc; the other 10 per cent consists of the police, who ride 250cc and above, businessmen, who have cars, and a few expats who have imported big bikes to ride at night when the police are asleep or drunk (either way they seem to get away with it pretty well). The chosen ride in the city is the Honda Steppy, either a real Honda or the model made under licence (or not) called the Dream. For those trendy young things with a bit more cash, there are the fancy plastic scooters.

Our first day involved a trip on two Honda Steppys at rush hour, when literally hundreds of thousands of bikes and scooters hit the streets. It's a truly amazing sight, and a baptism of fire. Dave and I were a tad over-excited at the prospect of joining what seemed to be complete traffic chaos. However, we were pleasantly surprised. When you're in such dense and chaotic traffic, everyone's riding takes on a Zen-like quality. The only thing I can liken it to is swimming with a shoal of fish. (Think about it: when was the last time you saw a shoal of fish crash in a mangled heap?) A similar rule applies to crossing the road. In any major city in Vietnam, the roads are so busy that to Western eyes there seems no possible way of doing it. However, with a leap of faith and a purposeful stride, lo, the traffic will avoid you. (The only exceptions to this are the minibus taxis. They pay little heed to anyone, and certainly not foreigners on foot or bikes.)

You should know that a bike in Vietnam is not just a form of transport for two people to pop down the shops. It is a regular sight to see Dad driving, his two children behind him, a new-born infant positioned in a basket over the front headlight, and Mam perched on the back holding Grandma, who is in turn holding the ashes of the recently deceased Grandad plus three live chickens and two carrier bags of goodies from the local market – all, I hasten to add, without helmets or any other kind of protection. Add to this their small family business delivering fish, live piglets, televisions and large panes of glass and you start to get an idea of motorcycling in Vietnam.

It had long been our intention to ride from Ho Chi Minh to Hanoi and then on to Ha Long Bay – some 2,400km. We had made several enquiries about doing the journey on larger bikes than the Hondas but hadn't come up with anything completely legal. If the film crew hadn't been about I know Dave and I would have gone for it, but the BBC takes a very dim view of that sort of thing so, as a last resort, we contacted a new-found mate. He promptly came up trumps and we went to meet him at a lock-up in downtown Ho Chi Minh, where he allegedly

190   V I E T N A M

had the very thing to suit our needs. We arrived in monsoon conditions, soaked to the skin but hopeful. The sign said SAIGON SCOOTER COMPANY. We were ushered in from the rain to a fanfare of 'Tadaaaa-h! Look at these beauties – superb or what!' We were looking at two 125cc single-cylinder 2-stroke Minsks, Russian-built kick-start strokers with drum brakes all round and large, comfy-looking seats finished in matt army green. Dave and I smiled. 'We'll have them.'

The ride back across the city on our new-found bikes was great fun. They didn't go very fast, they smoked like coal-fired power stations and handled like milk jelly, but they had great characters and we had access to the internals should the need to fiddle with them arise. Before we left, the boys at Saigon Scooters imparted some pretty sound advice for riding. The road law is strange in Vietnam and its enforcement even stranger. For instance, if you are involved in an accident, whether it's your fault or not, you will be charged as you are not Vietnamese and therefore, in theory, have access to more money, so are able to pay for any damage to body and bike, be it yours or a local's. Another tip: when stopped by the police, never hand over your passport. Corruption is rife and if you do hand it over you have given them an advantage when it comes to negotiating the bribe, normally about $20–$50. If they insist on seeing it, tell them you have left it at your hotel and ask them to escort you back there. Above all, don't panic: look at paying the bribe as a road toll and, whatever you do, don't take the moral high ground – that will be as popular as a fart in a spacesuit.

The next day, we decided we had to reach Hoi An, come hell or high water. When we finally got there, we arranged to meet the film crew at the ancient Chinese bridge that spans a tributary of the river to shoot a cookery bit. We arrived to set up our stall, planning to feed the ladies that work at the sampans. Now, in this area you tend to see a lot of French tourists on the trail of their fine country's colonial past. On this occasion my attention was captured by a particularly attractive Frency fancy, dressed in a flowing white dress and perfectly accessorised. I smiled and fluttered at her as only a large Geordie can. I was getting the bits together for the cookery, she was smiling at me now …Ohh, she's coming over, ohh, what will I say, my French is pants and I need to impress …Well, I hadn't got the first French riff out of my mouth when I fell arse over elbow into the gutter, fracturing my right ankle. Funny how fickle you become when in pain; I couldn't have cared if it had been Isabelle Adjani with her kit off.

I was promptly taken to the local hospital in a speeding convoy of rickshaws. Arriving at A&E, I was greeted by a very nice nurse, who prodded my ankle to find out how much pain I was in. I responded with the correct amount of expletives, so was handed over to a hyperactive porter with a Formula 1 wheelchair. A race ensued around the corridors of the hospital and over the odd flowerbed to the X-ray suite, to be greeted by a radiologist, cigarette in mouth, who looked like he had had a bad night in a bar. He placed me on the X-ray table and proceeded to manipulate my foot into positions it did not want to go. I grabbed his lapels and looked him in the eyes in a way that conveyed my discomfort and

suggested he should not proceed with this course of action. It's funny, isn't it, how these looks transcend all language barriers. X-ray finally taken, the doctor announced that indeed I had fractured my ankle. The nice nurse then administered a very large dose of morphine, I smiled, said thanks, and drifted off into a world of peace and contentment.

The rest of that day I must confess is a bit of a haze. Any time I asked for something, all I got was another pill. I remember being on a train at some point and Dave feeding me dried squid, which tasted like an old trainer. On arrival at the train station in Hue, Dave and the crew had organised a rickshaw. I began to get very confused: Where was I? Where were the bikes? Why had I been on a train? What was I doing in a rickshaw? And what the hell were these new wheels attached to my backside? Dave commandeered a rickshaw, gave me a bowl of pho and took me back to the hotel. I took one of the lovely pills the nice nurse-lady had given me and drifted back to my special place.

Next day, we were doing a cookery outside the imperial palace in Hue. Ohh good, I was feeling all right and there was a cookery to do. The crew had very kindly put up umbrellas to protect the kitchen from the rain. I was in my wheelchair, stuck underneath the table, and Dave was soldiering on in the monsoon, deep-frying spring rolls. All of a sudden – KABBBOOOOOMMMMM! – there's hot oil all over Dave's face and all over me. Dave is doing a jig, shouting expletives and asking for water, and I can't work out why I can't get out of the way of the fat. Turned out some bugger had put the brakes on my wheelchair without my knowing, so I was left to shuffle in my chair covered in hot oil, an experience I would not like to repeat.

NOODLE SALAD
With Lemongrass Dressing

We used the famous handmade coa lau noodles that you can only get in Hoi An. (Well, we can show off now and again.) This is a great accompaniment to the Hoi An crispy beef, as the lemon cuts into the beef a treat. Don't worry about serving hot and cold dishes together; the Vietnamese don't, and it gives yet another texture and dimension to their cuisine.

Serves 6

500g dried noodles, or the equivalent
  of fresh

the dressing

1 stick of lemongrass, smashed and
  chopped finely

juice of 2 lemons or limes

4 tbs sake

6 tbs nuoc cham sauce (see recipe
  on page 198)

Cook the noodles as per the instructions and leave them to cool. Mix together all the dressing ingredients, then, about half an hour before serving, dress the noodles and work it through so that they are all coated.

NUOC CHAM DIPPING SAUCE

Nuoc mam, the Vietnamese fish sauce, is made from fermented anchovies and is similar but much lighter than the Thai version we are more used to. It works really well as a seasoning – much better than simply adding salt – and comes in different strengths: 30, 40, 50 and 60 per cent. One step on from this is nuoc cham, which is everywhere in Vietnam, their version of ketchup. In fact it is sometimes referred to as 'universal sauce'.

In Vietnamese cooking you can use lemons or limes, depending on your taste, but just to confuse matters, in Vietnam the lemons are green…

50ml nuoc mam

100ml water

4 cloves of garlic, peeled and
  chopped finely

4 large chillies, chopped finely

50ml rice vinegar

50g caster sugar

juice of 1 lemon or lime,
  according to your taste

a garnish of carrot and cucumber,
  peeled and finely chopped

Simply combine all of the ingredients. Result: satisfaction guaranteed. Some recipes tell you to bring the sauce to a simmer (without the garnish, silly), to intensify the flavours. We have not found this necessary.

SOY DIPPING SAUCE

I love the way that the food is sometimes kept simple and all the alchemy goes into the dipping sauce. This one is great with the Hoi An crispy beef. It also works well with a simple roasted duck's breast, cutting through the fat like George Best through the opposition's defence.

200ml light soy sauce
1 clove of garlic, peeled and chopped finely
1 chilli, de-seeded and chopped finely
a thumb-sized piece of ginger, peeled and
    chopped finely

1 tspn sugar
1 tspn freshly ground black pepper
1 tbs peanuts, crushed
juice of 1 lemon

Mix all together!

STICKY TAMARIND DIPPING SAUCE

If you like citrus you'll love tamarind. The only thing to mention is that you need to use the pulp, not the black tasteless goo you get in most places. Oriental supermarkets sell it, as do numerous foodie websites, so there's no excuse.

1 chilli, chopped
4 tbs sake
1 tbs 30% nuoc mam
6 tbs orange juice

2 tbs water
4 tbs tamarind pulp
2 kaffir lime leaves, scrunched
palm sugar to taste

Place all the ingredients in a pan, heat and stir constantly. Taste and adjust sweetness with some palm sugar. Allow to reduce to the consistency of a runny conserve. Remove any tamarind stones and pour while warm into dipping bowls, then set aside to cool. Serve with our crab cakes.

CRYSTAL, OR RAW, SPRING ROLLS

Vietnamese spring rolls are the best in the world, and are what Vietnamese food is all about. All the levels of taste and texture are in this raw version, which looks brilliant. And when you dip them in nuoc cham sauce it's like lighting the touch paper on your taste buds: you bite through the firm rice-paper wrapper into the crunchy salad, then the sweet aromatic prawns – wow! – then you get a bang of hot chilli. Just as you think it's all over you get the cool coriander and spicy chives.

Makes 12

500g raw prawns, peeled and de-veined
200ml sake
600ml water
1 tspn honey mixed with hot water
12 rice papers
a handful of beansprouts
1 carrot, peeled and julienned
  (that is, cut into thin strips)
½ a cucumber, julienned too
2 large chillis, medium hot, de-seeded and
  julienned
bunch of chives, preferably the Vietnamese
  ones with flowers
bunch of coriander

In a pan, bring the water and sake to a slow simmer, pop in the prawns and poach for about 3 minutes. Don't overdo it: we want firm, happy, sake prawns, not dead men's toes. Take each rice paper and cut away two sides of it so that you are left with a 10cm rectangular strip rather than an circle.

Now the build. Take a clean cloth, dip it in the bowl of honey and water, and carefully moisten a rice paper. At one end put a few of the beansprouts, carrot and cucumber strips and roll over. Next put in a couple of the sake prawns and roll over again. (The reason for doing this is to give the different tastes and textures their own little compartments.) Then nip in a slice of chilli and roll, and finally some chives and coriander, leaving the stalks or flowers sticking out for that exclusive touch of Vietnamese style.

PRAWNS ON SUGARCANE

This is our take on a Vietnamese classic, finer than Pavarotti's tonsils. You get a wonderful mix of textures with the crispy sesame seeds and the tasty prawn mixture, and the sugarcane sweetness shoots all the way through the dish. At the end of the meal, give the sugarcane a chew – it's worth it. The pork is optional but it gives the dish a really juicy flavour.

Makes 10

500g raw prawns, peeled and de-veined

50g pork fat (optional)

100g dried shrimp, rehydrated and chopped fine

50g shallot, peeled and finely chopped

1 tbs nuoc mam

chilli, finely chopped, to taste

$\frac{1}{2}$ tspn freshly ground black pepper

10 sticks sugarcane

black and white sesame seeds

groundnut oil

to serve

nuoc cham dipping sauce

crispy salad

If you're using the pork fat, put it into a processor with the prawns and blend into a paste. Add the rehydrated shrimp, together with the shallot, fish sauce, chilli and black pepper, and blend again. This mixture will look like Technicolor wallpaper paste (this is a good thing).

Now for the artistic bit. Cut the sugarcane into sticks that look like lolly sticks at one end but are bigger and squarer at the other to hold the prawns. Wet your hands and mould a ball of the paste around the broad end of the cane, and smooth it so it looks like a egg- shaped lolly. Roll it in the mixture of sesame seeds, but don't make this a perfect coating – it's better if the sesame-seed coating is a bit hit and miss. Heat your oil and deep-fry on a medium rumble for about 5 minutes or until the prawns are coloured. If possible, finish these off over a charcoal fire to crisp them up and get a nice smoky flavour.

Serve on a bed of crispy salad with the nuoc cham dipping sauce.

PRAWNS POACHED
IN GREEN COCONUT

The fantastic vibe to this recipe is that it's so quick and simple but at the same time really impressive. We'll guarantee when you bring this dish to the table it is an event. Your guests will feast and love it, and if they don't, they clearly have no soul and should be left off the guest list for your next dinner party.

If you can't get green coconut (but make the effort, lazybones; you should be able to pick it up from your local Asian deli), pick up a whole coconut from the supermarket. You'll need to saw the top off it if you want to cook the dish in the shell but make sure you remove the milk first: pierce a hole with a skewer and drain the milk into a pan. Once you have taken the top off, pour the milk back into the coconut.

Serves 4

1 large green coconut
2 tspn ginger, peeled and roughly chopped
4 tspn galangal, roughly chopped
3 kaffir lime leaves
1 stick of lemongrass, bashed

1 large chilli, thinly sliced lengthways
1 tspn nuoc mam
16 raw crevettes, or the prawns of your choice (shell on if you prefer)

Slice the top off the green coconut (making sure you retain most of the milk in the process). Wrap the bottom of the coconut in aluminium foil. Place the ginger, galangal, lime leaves, lemongrass, chilli and fish sauce into the coconut with the remaining milk. Position your coconut over a medium gas flame and heat the broth through. If you have a camping stove, take this to the table and heat it up in front of your guests so they get the benefit of the fantastic aroma. When the broth is hot enough, drop your raw prawns in and wait until they go a lovely pink colour (about 3 minutes). Pick out the prawns carefully, eat and enjoy.

HA LONG CRAB AND WHITE FISH VERMICELLI SOUP With Ram Herb

The essence of this soup is the clear fish liquor. It really is fantastically delicate and the flavours are multi-layered and precise. It took my palate a while to adjust because it usually only recognises more robust flavours, but dear me when it got there – wow!

Don't be tempted to use the really hot chillies as they'll spoil the clarity of the soup.

Serves 6

2 live crabs (or 2 pre-cooked ones)
1 big slice of ginger
1 stick lemongrass, bashed
4 kaffir lime leaves, scrunched
½ shallot, peeled and chopped
a dash of nuoc mam
500g white fish fillets of your choice
200g vermicelli noodles, cooked and cut into manageable lengths

50g spring onion, finely chopped
1 large chilli (medium hot), cut lengthways and de-seeded
2 handfuls of fresh ram herb (or a mixture of fresh coriander and mint), chopped
1 lime, cut into wedges

to serve
nuoc mam
freshly ground black pepper

Put the crabs in a pan and cover with water. Add the ginger, lemongrass, lime leaves, shallot and a dash of fish sauce. Put the lid on and boil for 10–15 minutes. Turn off the heat, remove the crabs and set aside to let them cool. Put the white fish into the hot broth and leave them to cook in the remaining heat. Pick the crabs of meat, setting aside the white meat for the soup, and reserving the dark meat for your supper on hot, buttered toast.

Place the noodles in a serving bowl, add the spring onions, crab, chilli slice, ram and a lime slice. Bring the broth back to the boil and ladle over the serving bowl of ingredients, making sure you give everyone a piece of white fish.

Put the nuoc mam and pepper on the table so that guests can season to their own taste.

GRILLED FISH IN SPICES, CHA CA STYLE

This has been the signature dish at the Cha Ca La Vong restaurant in Hanoi for 900 years, so they should have got it right by now. It's a bit of a yin-yang balance of textures and flavours, and the method of double-cooking is a distinct Vietnamese thing. We cooked this on a charcoal fire in Ha Long Bay, one of the most beautiful places on the planet. You can use a very hot grill, and you might be pushed to get the fish as fresh as we did, but do give this one a go.

Makes 6

1kg firm white fish, such as bass, monkfish or halibut (we used the local catfish, hemibagrus, but try asking for that down the supermarket)

100g galangal, peeled and ground

50g turmeric root, peeled and ground

1 tspn shrimp paste

1 tspn freshly ground black pepper

3 tbs nuoc mam

groundnut oil

500g vermicelli rice noodles, cooked and cooled

150g peanuts, chopped and toasted

deep-fried banh da cracker

lime wedges

red chilli, de-seeded and finely sliced

200g spring onion, shredded

200g fresh dill

to serve

3 shallots, peeled and chopped finely

nuoc cham dipping sauce

Clean, scale and fillet the fish (or get the nice people at the fish counter to do it). Cut it into pieces about 5cm by 5cm, but it doesn't really matter – we won't call the fish police. In a bowl big enough to hold the fish, mix the ground-up galangal and turmeric. In a small bowl, dilute the shrimp paste with about 2 tablespoons of water. When the skanky bits have sunk to the bottom, skim the shrimp-paste water off the

top and add to the galangal and turmeric, then mix in the pepper and 1 tablespoon of the fish sauce. Marinate the fish for an hour or so in the resulting potion.

Preheat your grill so that it's very hot, and at the same time get the oil ready for deep-frying.

Take the fish out of the marinade, blot it with some kitchen paper, and grill, just to sear the outside. Then deep-fry the fish until it's cooked through. It will be a wonderful deep yellow. Set it aside. On a nice plate, place a portion of the cold noodles, dress with the rest of the nuoc cham sauce. Put the fish to the side of that, then, alongside that, the toasted peanuts. Crumble the crackers to another side and garnish with a slice of lime and chilli. At the last minute, deep-fry the spring onions and dill for about 30 seconds until they are wilted. Drape over the fish and serve.

HUE PADDY-FIELD PORK

Hue is famous for its imperial banquets and the flamboyant presentation of food. It must have been very stressful for a chef in those days, as the Emperor would readily murder anyone who did not please his palate. So, being the true revolutionaries we are, we decided to cook a good everyday recipe from the paddy-fields within the imperial citadel walls, with the hope that history on this occasion would not repeat itself.

Serves 4

100g light muscovado sugar

30ml of 60% nuoc mam diluted with 90ml water

500g pork loin, boned and diced

4 tbs shallot, peeled and chopped finely

4 kaffir lime leaves

4 cloves of garlic, peeled and chopped finely

1 tspn freshly ground black pepper

1 large chilli, sliced lengthways and de-seeded

juice of ½ a lime

4 quail's eggs, hard-boiled, shelled and halved

to garnish

4 cloves of garlic, peeled, sliced thinly and deep-fried

The caramel is a bit of a pain but is really worth the effort. You see, you want the colour and the taste of caramel, but not the full sweetness, so you need to get it to a dark gold, but not the full dark brown. So, put the sugar into a pan over a gentle heat, stir constantly and wait till it melts. You may need a little of the diluted fish sauce to help it on its way. Then let the colour darken, and slowly add the remainder of the diluted fish sauce until it all amalgamates.

Then add the pork, shallot, lime leaves, garlic, pepper, chilli and lime juice, cover and simmer on a slow heat for about 30 minutes, giving an occasional stir. If you like a thicker gravy, leave the lid off the pan for the last 10 minutes of cooking time.

Arrange the quail's eggs on a plate with the pork and pour some gravy on them. Garnish with the deep-fried garlic flakes and serve with sticky coconut rice.

STICKY COCONUT RICE

There is something really satisfying about sticky rice. You can roll it into a ball with a piece of meat, wrap it in a crispy leaf, top it with a rice cracker and put it in your mouth in one; the textures are amazing. It goes with many Asian dishes, not least our paddy-field pork. There is more starch in sticky rice than in a bishop's shirt, so wash it well to get rid of the excess, then soak it in plenty of water overnight. We have tried to cheat on this, but there are no short cuts.

Serves 6

500g glutinous (sticky) rice
100g finely grated coconut

Line a steamer with muslin, which keeps the rice from falling through the holes, then add the rice and the coconut. Steam for about 30 minutes, making sure that the pan doesn't boil dry. Serve in a natty little wicker basket for the true I've-been-to-Saigon sort of thing. Enjoy.

VIETNAMESE GARLIC MORNING GLORY

This is fabulous, a garlic-lover's delight. If you can't get morning glory (water spinach) at home, use pak choi or normal spinach. The cooking takes a minute, so have all your ingredients to hand.

Serves 6 as a side dish

2 tspn sesame oil
1 tbs groundnut oil
250g morning glory
6 small cloves garlic, whole

2 larger garlic cloves, peeled and chopped
1 tspn nuoc mam (or to taste)
freshly ground black pepper to taste

Put the oils in a wok and heat to a high temperature. Just before it starts to smoke, add the morning glory, all the garlic, the nuoc mam and pepper. Flash-fry for no longer than a minute, tossing all the ingredients together. Serve immediately.

HOI AN CRISPY BEEF

A familiar recipe, great to cook and eat, so get stuck in. Don't worry too much about how much galangal and ginger you use – all palates differ. You can put some chilli into the mix if you like, it really is up to you. Go on, experiment! (But avoid garlic because it will burn.) Serve this with the noodle salad with lemongrass dressing and soy dipping sauce.

Serves 4

for the marinade
2 eggs, beaten
1 tbs sesame oil
½ tspn palm sugar
2 tspn fresh galangal, sliced into strips
1 tbs fresh ginger, peeled and sliced
3 tspn sesame seeds
1 tbs nuoc mam
1 tspn of rice wine or sake
1 tspn freshly ground black pepper

500g fillet of beef, cut thinly across the grain
cornflour
sunflower or groundnut oil

Mix all the marinade ingredients together in a bowl and add the beef, letting it drink in all those great flavours – the longer you leave it the better it is.

Put the cornflour into a bowl. Then, in a suitable wok or pan, preheat 4cm of the oil until it is very hot and bubbling. Don't be tempted to put lots of beef into the oil at once, or it will end up like the sole of an old trainer. So, one strip at a time, blot the beef with kitchen paper, then dip it into the cornflour, covering the meat well. Drop into the hot oil, leave until crispy, then remove and drain.

EXOTIC FRUIT SALAD

There is nothing better than this on a hot humid day, or when you're fed up with winter comfort food and want a fresh taste to remind you of summer. This recipe is also an invitation to forage for fruits you wouldn't ordinarily buy. Take the kids and spend your Saturday morning in those riental shops you usually pass on your way to the shopping mall. It really is a more fulfilling experience asking the shopkeeper about what's for sale. Equally, you can use any combination of fruits you can get your hands on.

Depending on your lifestyle, leave the alcohol out so that you can serve what you don't eat for breakfast, or, if you leave it in, have it as an early morning livener.

Serves 4

1 dragonfruit (these are a great pinky-red colour with wisps growing out of them, a bit like a flaky pink, hand grenade)

8 rambutan (little red beauties with hair all over them)

4 lychees

1 papaya

2 kiwi

2 Chinese pears

1 tsp palm sugar (or to taste)

juice of 1 lime

sake or vodka (optional)

Prep the fruit with your newly found knowledge. Melt the palm sugar in the lime juice and pour over the fruit. Pour over your sake or vodka if you like, and serve.

VIETNAMESE CARAMELISED BANANAS

This is one of those desserts that you can't stop eating and is great served with real vanilla or coconut ice cream. Go on, be a devil, you know you want to!

Serves 4

4 bananas
200g Japanese breadcrumbs
100g cashew nuts, crushed
groundnut oil

4 tbs water
4 drops vanilla extract
300ml coconut milk
2 tspns desiccated coconut (optional)

the caramel sauce
20g butter
150g soft brown sugar

to serve
lime
ice cream

It is really lovely to infuse the coconut milk with a vanilla pod the night before you cook this dish, then scrape the seeds into the milk before you make the caramel sauce with it. If you don't remember in time, vanilla extract is just as good.

Peel and quarter the bananas lengthways and role them firmly in the Japanese breadcrumbs and cashew nuts so they stick. Set aside.

Heat together all the ingredients for the sauce until a golden-brown colour is achieved. Leave to cool. Deep-fry the bananas until the breadcrumbs turn a light golden colour. Put the banana on a plate and pour the caramel to the side so you retain the crunch. Serve with a wedge of lime and ice cream of your choice.

MEXICO

MEXICO CITY

OAXACA   SAN CRISTOBAL   PALENQUE
          DE LAS CASAS

          TUXTLA
          GUTIERREZ

Mexico

'Mexico is divided into thirty or so states, each with its own
flavour. As a whole, it is one of the most colourful, hospitable
countries in the world. We wanted to find the traditional Mexico,
as far from American influences as possible, to discover the
indigenous people and to look for pre-Hispanic food.'

DAVE: What a country! Mexico is huge, almost 2 million square kilometres and covering three time zones. It is bordered by California, Arizona, New Mexico and Texas to the north, Belize and Guatemala to the south, the Pacific to the west and the Gulf of Mexico and the Caribbean to the east. It's hot and steamy in the coastal jungle regions and freezing cold in the highlands, which run for thousands of kilometres along its spine and are home to 3,000 volcanoes, many still active. These geographical extremes and seismic instabilities, together with a seriously old, complex culture, give Mexico its unique character.

Mexico is divided into thirty or so states, each with its own flavour. As a whole, it is one of the most colourful, hospitable countries in the world. We wanted to find the traditional Mexico, as far from American influences as possible, to discover the indigenous people and to look for pre-Hispanic food. We concentrated on two states, Oaxaca and Chiapas, beginning in Oaxaca City and working our way south towards Guatemala, ending up in the ancient Mayan city of Palenque. We also found a route that gave us one of the best motorcycling trips you could wish for.

First a bit of history. About 6,000 BC, desert nomads began to settle in Mexico, cultivating corn, chillies and squashes. The mother of all ancient cultures, the Olmecs ('People from the Land of Rubber'), prospered, leaving behind 3-metre high, 20-ton carved heads, which appear to be wearing really crap crash helmets, all over the country. The Olmecs fizzled out about 600 BC and were superseded by the Zapotecs, the Toltecs and the Mixtecs. The Aztecs appeared around AD 1300 and became the last rulers of a Mexican empire. They were all highly sophisticated cultures and left us their ruined cities and pyramids, from which we get clues as to how they lived. The Mayans were experts at mathematics and astronomy, had their own system of hieroglyphics and worshipped the feathered serpent. They played ball games which often ended with the losers being decapitated. (Maybe they should introduce that at St James's Park – that would get Newcastle to the top of the table!) In 1487, at the height of the Aztec empire, 20,000 captives were sacrificed at the dedication of the great pyramid, their beating hearts torn from their bodies by priests. The gods were fed and the Aztecs had ensured the continuity of the cosmos.

It would have been amazing to be a fly on the wall at an Aztec court. However, like all good things, something had to change. Columbus arrived in 1492 on a mission to find spices, amongst other things (remember, it was these explorers who brought chillies from Central and South America and gave them to the Far East). In 1517, Don Cortés and about 600 Conquistadores arrived and conquered the nation. They had a different agenda: gold. It was the start of 300 years of Spanish rule that would bring the decline of the indigenous population, and the introduction of Christianity and a land-owning system that has its repercussions today. It wasn't till Napoleon invaded Spain in 1808 and revolutionary ideas spread throughout the world that Mexico declared war on Spain and finally got its independence in 1821. The final invaders, just as damaging, were the 'Gringos', who arrived in 1846 and forced Mexico to cede New Mexico, Texas and California to America.

Down south where we went, around Oaxaca and Chiapas, the American influence is minimal and you can find the true Mexico. Descendants of the various 'tec' peoples are still there, and the ancient languages still spoken. We fell in love with this part of the country, its food and its people. They have a huge zest for life, and with more than 4,000 fiestas a year you are never short of a knees-up.

SI: There was nothing we did not like about Mexico – its people, its climate, its roads, the food, the architecture and the markets. And the route we settled on took in some of the best roads and scenery Mexico has to offer. The landscape varies dramatically, from the mountains of the Sierra Madre to the large central plateaus and jungle in the south and east. We always knew the food was going to be interesting, but, as we discovered, it was completely fantastic and diverse. Wherever we have ridden, the scenery and food seem to define that country's people and cuisine and Mexico was no exception.

Oaxaca ('Wah-hock-uh') has got everything: great weather, great street-life and great buildings. None of the houses are more than two floors high and they're all painted different colours. Mexican colours, that is. You can't wait to get home and paint the front of your house turquoise or pink (but don't try this, dear reader, you'll only look a prat!). The narrow cobbled streets are laid out in a grid system, so navigation was at first glance relatively easy; however, a sprinkle of one-way systems soon put paid to that. But we didn't mind getting lost: there's brilliant street food on every corner, a mezcal bar on every block and the sound of marimba in the air. It's heaven for a northern lad.

As in all Mexican towns, the market is fantastic. There are about 300 types of chilli and you can get them all at a single stall. And the magical sits side by side with the mundane; right by the stand selling leather boots and belts, there's a booth selling little packets of powder made from 'authentic intestines of demons' to put in your enemy's hot chocolate, or 'legitimate powder of German' to make your lost lover come back to you.

Oaxaca gets its name from the Aztec settlement of Huaxyacac, meaning 'Nose of the Squash' – a perfect place, then, to do some cooking. Oaxaca's a modern city, even though it's full of reminders of the Spanish colonial past. At its centre is the usual big plaza with a bandstand, and all day long the world passes through. Nowt like a quiet location! We had a traditional mariachi band to accompany our delectable dishes and Dave and I got involved in a somewhat strange rendition of 'La Bamba'. We must have looked quite a sight: we'd got all excited and bought some really cool Mexican gear our first day – ponchos, cowboy hats, boots and shirts, the usual stuff. We thought it must be really good cos it cost so much – but after walking about town for another day or two we realised they'd been having a laugh. Still, we got to strut around dressed like heavies in a Spaghetti Western (and I tell you what, you pull up on a couple of major Harleys dressed like that, and you pull!).

DAVE: We like cooking in the open air and in the middle of things if possible. For some reason, probably not unconnected with the fact we were having a chilli cook-off in the equivalent of the fountains of Trafalgar Square, complete with guitars, we seemed to be drawing a crowd. There was this beautiful woman hanging around near the bandstand, looking admiringly up at us. She had the curves of a goddess and a sweet smile full of secrets. We thought it would be nice if she came up onto the bandstand when we were done and maybe joined us dancing to 'La Bamba', so we sent our producer to sort it out. He came back with a worried look in his eye. 'Boys, nice girls in Mexico are not called "Lady" and they certainly don't dress like that!' Then the representative of the local film commission came up. Why were we trying to invite a well-known working girl up onto the platform with us? The last we saw of 'Lady' she was going off with two hopeful-looking young Americans. I guess we'll never know if that was her real name.

Mexico has great beer, but in Oaxaca the drink is mezcal and we met several great producers. Some do it on an industrial scale, but we found a small producer who was still making it in the traditional way. On our first night in Oaxaca we checked into our hotel. About an hour later there was a knock on the door and Si stood there, slightly wobbly.

'You all right, mate?'
'Bin fer a walk, found a mezcal bar, come on, mate, we've got you one in!'
'Cowabunga! Let us get me shoes on.'

We went to the bar of Don Francisco, a temple to mezcal, where Si had seized on the hospitality like a Jack Russell around your leg. Everything that was for sale in the bar had been made by Don Francisco. As our eyes got used to the dark, glassy-eyed grinning faces appeared. Ah well, they all seemed happy enough. Let's give it a shot!

SI: Mezcal is different to tequila in that tequila must only be made from the blue agave plant, while mezcal can be made from a combination of agaves. Drinking mezcal is not so much a means of getting smashed as a revered ritual, much as one drinks good malt whisky. Don Francisco's bar was a lesson in flavour diagnosis as the liquor swirled and whooshed over our tastebuds. Some were slightly smoky, some very young with a clean, green finish, but all of them were wonderful – a better bet then tequila for my money. It turns out that only the lower end mezcal comes with that worm at the bottom. There are as many grades and vintages of mezcal as there are of whisky, and the top end doesn't need any gimmicks.

DAVE: I had a lovely smooth Anjeho, an aged mezcal which you drink with a bite on a lime and some grasshopper salt which is a mixture of ground-up grasshoppers, salt and chilli. Next we tried a new, light mezcal, then a fruit mezcal and one with the worm in. The world was rapidly becoming a rosy, cuddly, scrumptious place. We had to find out more and Don Francisco kindly invited us to his distillery. What a wonder awaited us. It was in the middle of a plantation of agave and the mountains stretched out into the distant horizon. A donkey harnessed to a mill walked with slow purpose, crushing the agave underneath a large, round stone set on its end, like an ancient wheel from the time of the Mayans and Aztecs. The perfume in the air was a mixture of wood-smoke and natural sugar slowly fermenting in the vats, the sky and mountains perfectly reflected in their stillness. We had found heaven and a true sense of Mexico.

After our wonderful introduction to the country we were off to Tuxtla Gutiérrez in the state of Chiapas. There was anticipation in the air as we rode; we knew that we were entering a state that was passionate about its historical and cultural identity. In 1994 the Zapatista rebels occupied a town on our route called San Cristóbal de las Casas. They were led by the balaclava-wearing, pipe-smoking Subcomandante Marcos. Their beef was with the government's failure to deliver a fair deal on land rights to the indigenous people, and the corrupt way local state government was run. In response the

Mexican authorities sent in huge numbers of troops and set up checkpoints to make their presence felt. In typical Mexican style the local people thought, 'What a set of daffties,' and got on with their daily routines.

Dave and I arrived at our first checkpoint, showed papers, smiled and left – much better than the experience we had in Turkey. Arriving in Tuxtla itself was a bit of a non-event so we decided to ride on up to the nearby Canyon del Sumidero. The canyon is as spectacular as we had heard. The scale and serenity of the place really does take your breath away – and we had found yet another cookery site.

DAVE: Tuxtla is Ground Zero for chocolate, which the Mayans and Aztecs believed was a gift of their gods. Si and I parked ourselves up a cliff overlooking the stunning Canyon del Sumidero and cooked the world's best hot chocolate. To make the basic chocolate you simply grind cocoa beans along with sugar to taste and some almonds and cinnamon. You can make about two kilos of the stuff for about £7. We bought a molinillo, another Spanish invention, a sort of wooden whisk for frothing up your hot chocolate. It tasted the best. We toasted the Aztec gods with it whilst thanking the Spanish for adding some sugar.

SI: Yet another beautiful sunrise and off to Chiapa de Corzo and a PARTY! Well, a fiesta to be precise, of St Sebastian (the camp dude with lots of arrows in him, as Dave so eloquently put it). We donned our ponchos, bought a couple of masks and stood and jigged on the spot to the numerous bands that past. Then suddenly a big old Mexican woman in the parade grabs us by the hands and pulls us into the dancing horde, spins us around, shows us some steps and there's a roar from the crowd! We're dancing like maniacs, and the people are with us. Turns out we'd melted into the crowd like two gorillas

at a duck farm. Everyone had been watching us and when we joined the parade, they loved it. That's the thing about Mexico. It's such a welcoming culture. They celebrate life and they want you to feel at home: *mi casa es su casa*, our parade is your dance floor! Mind you, after our turn the next big cheer from the crowd came at the appearance of two more dancers behind us, one dressed as King Kong, the other as Zorro. So maybe they thought we were film stars!

DAVE: The next day we were off to San Cristobel. The roads are fantastic, the views amazing; it was perfect biking. Given our new enthusiasm for dance, we booked ourselves into a salsa class at the local cultural centre. We stood outside the entrance and watched as lots of Latin lovelies went into the class to strut their stuff. We walked in and the people could not have been nicer. One of the teachers had an hourglass figure and moved like a fruit sorbet – ye know, all cool and slippy. Please pick us to teach, please! And she did …

Now enough of that. I was in need of some spiritual cleansing and a new-found mate from the salsa class suggested we visit a shaman. We were taken to his home, little more than a shack but dignified, and the ceremony started. The chant resonated to the point where it seemed to go to the very core of your being. I remember very little after that, other than the amazing feeling I was left with when all was over. I find it difficult to put the experience into words except to say that I was in the presence of something wonderful and felt very privileged to be given such an opportunity.

SI: And then on to Palenque, one of the great archeological sites of the world. The further south we went, the more we saw the signs of the old ways, and our final cookery plan was to make something that the ancient Maya would recognise. Palenque has an air of serenity and defiance, a wonderful place to end a journey and to reflect on the experiences Dave and I had had on the road over the previous year.

DAVE: Si and I sat at the top of one of the Palenque pyramids listening to a chorus of unfamiliar birds chattering away, under a frieze showing one of the lords of Palenque receiving homage from his prisoners. We had one of those quiet moments of reflection.

We thought about how far we'd travelled in the past year and how many places we'd explored, how many strangers had befriended us and how many food adventures we'd had. Well, that's what I was thinking about. With that mad Geordie glint in his eye, Si breaks into my reverie, rubbing his hands together and licking his chops. 'Now, Dave, we're here at the top of the Palenque pyramid. Those Mayans pioneered blood sacrifice and ate the living hearts of their victims. Do you think one of these carvings might have a good recipe on it?' Oh, Si, what are you like! But I'm game to go along for the ride…

FOOD BITS

DAVE: Mexicans care about food, and it is a wonderful, deep food culture, thousands of years old. So much is unique, like the string cheese of Oaxaca, and, as in Vietnam, it was nice to find a cuisine that isn't wheat dependent. Mexico was the perfect end to our grand odyssey. When we started in Portugal we found so many influences from the New World; in Mexico we found the source of a lot of those everyday foods.

Chillies (or chilis, as the Mexican people call them) are one of the building blocks of Mexican cooking. The heat of a chilli is due to the capsicum that is in the veins and seeds, which are always removed so you have more control of the heat in the dish (in Mexico, a dish that is too hot to enjoy is the sign of a bad chef). Chillies are also good for you. They are high in vitamins C and A and also contain vitamins E, B1, B2 and B3. The Aztecs realised their medicinal qualities and used them to cure digestive and respiratory problems, as well as earache and toothache. I think that they just make you feel good. If chillies be the spice of life…bring it on!

Chillies are not simply a hot hit. There are more than 300 varieties, each with a different taste and strength, from which you build a palette for each dish. They can be used as seasoning, made into a salsa or served as a dish in themselves, such as chilis Rellenos (stuffed chillies) or a bowl of lightly stewed chipotle chillies which gives you a remarkable smoky, aromatic side dish. In Oaxaca we visited a chilli dealer, where sacks of dried chillies sat like bags of coal and the scent took your breath away. The dealer can't even shake your hand as his are so infused with chillies they would burn you. The strongest are the pequin chillies, about the size of a hazelnut. They are as hot as Hades and are used as the base for Tabasco sauce. In the UK we get another hot one, the habanero chilli, which we know as scotch bonnet chillies. These also found their way to the Caribbean, where they are the favourite; in Mexico they are used mostly for salsa. The ancho chillies lie like old socks after a long bike ride, juicy and full of aroma.

Now, you don't just throw the chillies into a dish. Dried chillies must be split, the seeds and veins removed, and then dry-roasted on a comal, a concave clay dish, or a cast-iron frying pan till they're blistered. (Mind your eyes while you're doing this, it's the same as police using pepper spray!) Then plunge them into boiling water to rehydrate them and use them as required. There are two main types of fresh chillies: serrano and jalapeño. The Mexicans often toast these too, but make sure you pierce them first so they don't explode. Once toasted, split and take out the seeds and the veins. These are great for salsas.

The other great staple in Mexico is corn. Historian Eusebio Dávalos Hurtado has found over 700 recorded Mexican recipes for corn. And it has its roots in the very fibre of the people. According to their holy book, Popol Vuh, when the Mayans were created the gods first tried to use clay and wood, but the clay wasn't strong enough and the wood lacked soul. The perfect

balance was found in a blend of yellow and white corn, ground and formed into the great Mayan race. Babies are still called 'maize blossoms', young girls 'tender green ears' and an able warrior 'Lord King Cobb'.

A Mexican housewife would start making the masa, the cornmeal dough, the day before it's needed. It goes like this: you get some corn (not sweetcorn; this is a variety that looks like giant teeth), add some lime – that's the powdered rock, not the fruit – boil it for one hour, then leave it overnight. This is to break down the husk. The next day you sit with a metete, a rectangular piece of rock, and with a mano, a rock rolling pin, and start to grind the corn with water into a paste. By the time you have done this you will have some great dough and shoulders like a bison. Alternatively you can take it to the local mill, the molina, which has a big electric grinder, and for a peso they will grind the corn in about thirty seconds. All towns have a molina and they provide yet another setting for the Mexican love of socialising and chat. What a great start to the day.

Now you have your dough, you make your daily bread, the tortilla. Fresh tortillas are lovely, a world away from the pre-packed bags of sog that we get in the UK. And once you have them, a cornucopia of recipes opens up before your very eyes. Of course, you can just eat them as they are, dipped in a lovely salsa, but you can also cut them into wedges and fry them (nachos), melt some cheese on top for cheesy nachos, sandwich two together with a filling of your choice, toast them and have quesadillas, take a massive one and build up a tlayuda, stuff them and fry them for tacos, or make enchiladas (a kind of cannelloni roll with salsa on top), chalupas (a boat-shape tortilla stuffed with beans and cheese) or make the little pasties called empanadas. Memelitas are also nice, but one of our favourites is tetelas, the samosa-like tortilla parcel that we cooked in the bandstand in Oaxaca.

'Mexico is also the land of chocolate. The Aztecs used to offer
it to the gods in the hope of maintaining amicable relations.
(I wonder if this is why on Valentine's Day you give your girl a
box of chocolates – "Egh, love...any chance of amicable relations!")'

The other great favourite that you get on all street corners is the tamale, where you make a
parcel with various salsas and sometimes pieces of meat, roll them in a corn husk or
a banana leaf and then steam them. (This steamed masa meal is really just the same as
polenta. We know that chillies came to Europe from Mexico and South America; did polenta
start as a tamale and then become mamaliga in Romania? These anthropological food
threads keep reappearing...) Women spend hours making them for family celebrations, and
they're a great festival food, given as offerings to the gods. Tamales are not easy to make well.
On our trips there have been several times when you get a moment where gastronomically,
food doesn't get any better, and very often the amazing food has not been in fine restaurants
but on the streets. We met an old lady outside a mezcal bar in Oaxaco who sold three types
of tamale: chicken with a verde (green coriander) sauce, chicken with a dark mole sauce
(we will go into that later) and one with beans and herba-santa sauce (which tastes of
sarsaparilla). This was a food epiphany for me, some of the best things I have ever tasted,
with generations of skill and decades of daily practice in each one. That's where the bikes
really came into their own: to find the good stuff you need to be out on the streets.

Mexico is also the land of chocolate. The Aztecs used to offer it to the gods in the hope of maintaining amicable relations. (I wonder if this is why on Valentine's Day you give your girl a box of chocolates – 'Egh, love…any chance of amicable relations!') The cocoa bean was so highly regarded that the beans were used as currency. Ten beans could buy a rabbit, a hundred beans a slave. You could also pay your taxes with them, and even then scallywags would try to slip in fake cocoa beans made from clay or carved avocado stones. When the Spanish arrived and tried the hot chocolate, it was so bitter they couldn't keep it down. Wisely, they added cane sugar, milk, almonds and cinnamon to the bitter broth, which gives us the base for the chocolate that we have today. By the beginning of the seventeenth century, chocolate had made its way back to the Spanish court. Soon, chocolate consumption had reached addictive proportions (there are records of one unfortunate friar who was brought before the Inquisition for drinking chocolate before celebrating mass). By the late seventeenth century, it had spread to England. Pepys writes about going down to his local chocolate house for his first drop of the day; White's club in St James's was once White's Chocolate House. And the English can take the credit for the first eating chocolate when Fry's of Bristol made the first bar in the nineteenth century, followed by Cadbury's a few years later. So, when you're munching yours, remember the Mayans.

The national dish in Mexico is mole ('mol-é'), which simply means mixture (indeed 'guaca-mole' is the simplest form made from avocados). There can be up to fifty ingredients, and each variation produces a unique taste. Mexicans take the dish very seriously; there is even an annual mole festival south of Mexico City. The original recipe is said to have come from Oaxaca state. The story goes that in the convent of Santa Rosa in Puebla, one of the nuns was trying to please a visiting bishop. All the nuns had a say in what went into the dish, hence the large number of ingredients. The crowning glory was the addition of chocolate, a precious commodity fit for such an important visitor. When you get to our recipe for mole Pueblana (a mole negro), you'll see it's a complex and time-consuming dish, but it's worth the effort. The blend of chillies gives the dish various levels of taste and the roasting of the vegetables and fruit create a unique taste. Other popular moles are the mole verde, which is full of coriander and fresh-tasting, the mole coloradito, a red mole, not as sharp as the negro, the mole amarillo, which is thickened with corn, the mole rojo, red and tasty, the mole mancha manteles, made with pineapple, and lastly the mole chichilo, which is sharpened by burning chilli seeds on the top of a tortilla. Making moles is fun.

Finally, there are lots of crickets in Mexico. Or is it grasshoppers? Not hopping, though. Not jumping or flying either. Deep-fried with chillies and lying there in huge heaps in the markets or on wide bowls carried on the heads of street vendors. They're a favourite snack in southern Mexico. They're piled up according to size and you eat them in handfuls, like peanuts. And they pop up in lots of dishes. My favorite is fundido, which is a bowl of melted cheese full of chilli-fried crickets. Lots of protein!

BIKE BITS

Si: We flew into Puebla, south of Mexico City, and hurried in anticipation (despite the hideous jet lag) to pick up the bikes from a local dealership. At this point we didn't know what we were getting other than the make, Harley-Davidson (well, wouldn't you if you had the chance?). The orange and black sign of the dealership popped out of the faceless facade of the street, just as it does the world over, and we walked through the doors into the sanitised and standardised 'Live to Ride, Ride the Dream' formula. (Never mind: they were kind enough to lend us the bikes!) We were desperate to find out which models we had been allocated for the show, and there they were. It took us a while to see past the sunlight reflected in the chrome but we donned our shades and gawped. 'Have they really lent us these?' Dave asked. 'Must have, mate, they've got our names on them.' Dave had been allocated a beautiful burgundy Road King, ideal for the trip, and I was on a Heritage Softail Deluxe, both bikes boasting the new 1450cc engines. My bike was in black and white with a thin red pinstripe, so we called it the TOON ARMY HARLEY! We thanked the lads at the dealership and tootled back to the hotel with our new steeds, looked at them for a bit in the car park, then stumbled upstairs and promptly fell asleep as the jet lag hit us.

Morning soon came and we prepared to hightail it to Oaxaca, some four hours' ride. We roared out of the car park and took a tight left-hander. Dave's bike coped no problem; mine went to ground with a spectacular display of sparks. 'Nice one, Kingy.' 'What was that, mate? It didn't feel like a footplate or side-stand.' On further investigation we found that it had been the frame; the ground clearance on the bike was awful and it would not lie down in a bend. We knew from having owned Harleys the type of client that buys this bike – you know, paid off the mortgage, kids have grown up, worked hard all their lives and want something for themselves. And good for them, I say. However, this was a bike for straight lines and a weekend tootle down to the local coffee bar, not for a 2,000km rampage on some of the most mountainous, twisty roads any self-respecting biker could wish for. Hey ho, I was stuck with her and her livery was black and white after all. During the trip we seemed to work each other out. She couldn't stop as she only had one small disc and what looked like a chrome jelly mould on the front, she hated corners and the ninety-degree bends we encountered needed approaching with the utmost caution, but we got the measure of each other and managed an average of 60kph through the mountain passes – not bad for a bike that hates corners. The new engines were as torquey as you would expect but did not seem to give any extra power – but then again both Dave and I own Italian bikes, so exceptional power delivery was not an expectation.

On our route to Oaxaca we encountered the topes, the Mexican equivalent of speed humps, but really more hills than humps. They are a bloody menace but effective. Just to catch you out at night or at dusk they do not signpost them, so you arrive on said hump with screeching brakes and a look in your eye suggesting that pain is imminent in your nether regions as the bike comes up to meet them. They tend to be positioned on the way into and out of any city, town or village, so approaching one of these at night (look out for the lights of houses near the side of the road) with caution and low speed will save you a stay in the local hospital. Every road-user treats them with the utmost respect – a far better deterrent than the nannying speed cameras we find ourselves with in the UK.

The Mexican landscapes are magnificent: from huge canyons and high mountains, mad with flowers and eagles, to big rivers crossing hot dusty plains. There are some fantastic biking roads. The driving attitude in Mexico is good and courteous. Having thought about why this should be different to other countries we've visited, I have come to the conclusion that Mexicans are cautious people on the roads, perhaps because of the complete lack of state healthcare, so the last thing they want to do is park their bodies all over the tarmac. The vehicles you should watch out for are the newer cars, perhaps on the basis that their owners have more money and can afford healthcare, so drive more aggressively. However, overall they are more likely to wave at you than knock you off.

There are a few basics you need to master for Mexican cooking: the tortilla, refried beans, a few simple salsas and guacamole. So we're going to give you those recipes before moving on to the more complicated stuff. But first you need a few supplies, namely a tortilla press, some masa meal, a good selection of chillies. You can find all of these from specialist suppliers, mostly online. As a good start, have a look at the Cool Chile Co. (*www.coolchile.co.uk*), *www.chillipeppersonline.co.uk* and the South Devon Chilli Farm (*www.southdevonchillifarm.co.uk*).

TORTILLAS

As you know now, if you can make one of these you can eat them as a side dish, toast them and make quesadillas, fry them to make tacos, top them with cheese for nachos, or stuff them and make enchiladas. The list goes on…It's great grub.

Makes about 12 x 15cm tortillas

225g masa meal
285ml water

In a processor or by hand, mix the masa meal with enough water so that it looks like a ball of window putty. Next cut two 15cm discs from a plastic bag and place one on your tortilla press. Then place a golf ball of masa meal on the plastic, cover with the other circle of plastic and pump the press gently. With a bit of practice you will have a disc of dough about the thickness of a beer mat. In Mexico they cook these on a hot comal, which you put directly onto the gas flame or wood fire. You can use a heavy cast-iron pan, with no oil, to the same effect. Cook the tortilla for a few minutes on either side until it begins to brown and puff up, and there you have it: your first home-made tortilla. Now, let the fun begin.

REFRIED BEANS

This is real cowboy food. You need to soak the beans overnight in plentiful water, then drain and boil them in fresh water. We like the taste the smoky bacon gives us, but you could try ordinary bacon – or of course, if you're a veggie, no bacon at all!

Serves 6–8

500g black or pinto beans
1.4 litres water
2 tbs olive oil
a knob of butter

1 medium onion, peeled and chopped fine
250g smoked streaky bacon, chopped into
    matchstick-sized pieces

Boil the beans till tender, then reserve the water. Next, in a large frying pan, heat the oil and butter and sweat down the onion for a few minutes. Add the bacon and fry until it's cooked through. Now mash the beans as fine as you want and mix them with the bacon-onion mixture. Add some of the reserved cooking water to give you the consistency that you like. We think it's best kinda like double cream.

TETELAS DE HAIRY BIKERS

Armed with our new-found ability to make tortillas, refried beans (see pages 234–5) and the essential salsas and guacamole (page 238–9), we're off to make tetelas, sort of triangular tortilla turnovers. We've given you two different fillings and these amounts will make about 6 of each. There'll be some meat left over, but hey, it's cook's perks and you'll want to nibble as you go. Serve the finished tetelas on sliced crispy lettuce, with a dollop of the guacamole on one side and one of the raw salsa on the other. Oh, and an ice-cold Mexican beer on yet another side works well too. Arriba, arriba!

Serves 6

1 x quantity of masa dough
1 x quantity of refried beans
100g pecorino cheese
100g gouda cheese
100g Cheddar cheese

for the chicken one
2 chicken breasts
1 lime, sliced
2 chipotle chillies (the smoked ones)

for the pork one
500g pork loin
1 apple, peeled, cored and sliced

Preheat the oven to 180°C. Slit the chicken breasts halfway through, place a chilli and a couple of slices of lime in each slash, season well and wrap them loosely in a foil parcel. Bake in the oven for 45 minutes.

Slash the pork two or three times (this helps it bake more evenly) and give it a good hammering with a mallet or the end of a rolling pin. Put the meat in the centre of a large piece of foil, pile slices of apple around it and make another loose parcel. Bake in the oven for 30 minutes.

Meanwhile, warm through the refried beans, and grate the three cheeses into a bowl. When the meat's done, make a tortilla disc (it's quite delicate, so handle carefully) and put a tablespoon of refried beans in the middle. Top with some slices of chicken – about a tablespoon full – then sprinkle with a tablespoon of grated cheese. Fold three sides of the tortilla over to make a triangular shape, but leave a hole in the middle – think samosa with the sides not quite meeting.

Heat your comal or dry cast-iron frying pan on the hob, then place the tetela cheese-side down on the pan and toast for about 5 minutes, then for 5 minutes on the other side. Don't worry if the cheese oozes out of the hole and burns; this makes it very yummy and tasty. Repeat with the apply pork.

REAL GUACAMOLE

This is a traditional guacamole and is quite runny, very different to the Tex-Mexy one we did in the Isle of Man. It goes really well with the tetelas and salsas. Imagine the lovely green colour with the bright red salsa and the yummy toasted treats…Eeh, I'm making meself hungry.

Serves 6

1 onion, peeled and finely chopped
4 mild chillies, de-seeded and
   finely chopped
a bunch of coriander, chopped
2 tomatoes, peeled and finely diced
salt to taste

2 tbs water
2 tbs lime juice
3 avocados, peeled, halved and stoned

In a processor or a pestle and mortar (or a molcajete), blend the onion, chillies, coriander, tomato and salt to a fine paste. Add the water and lime juice to make a loose paste, mash in the avocado and serve.

HOT CHILLI SALSA

This goes great with the green rice and super-tasty pre-Hispanic stew.

Serves 6

3 hot chillies (Scotch bonnet say), pierced
250g whole plum tomatoes
4 whole garlic cloves
1 red bell pepper
juice of $\frac{1}{2}$ a lime
salt to taste

Heat your comal or dry cast-iron frying pan on the hob and roast the chillies, then de-seed and de-vein them. Next roast the tomatoes, garlic and the sweet red pepper, then skin them. Blend the whole lot together in a processor and add the lime juice and seasoning.

RAW SALSA

This is a really fresh uncooked salsa, very different to the other saucy cooked salsas. It goes really well with the tetelas on page 237.

Serves 6

250g plum tomatoes, peeled
1 small onion, peeled
3 mild chillies, de-seeded
a bunch of coriander, finely chopped

salt to taste
lime juice to taste
1 tbs water

Chop the tomatoes and onion into a small, even dice, and chop the chillies very finely. Combine all the ingredients and serve as soon as possible.

GREEN SALSA

This is a dry-roasted salsa with green chillies that is simple to make and lovely with tortilla chips and sour cream.

Serves 6

3 plum tomatoes
$\frac{1}{2}$ a medium onion, peeled
6 cloves of garlic, peeled
4 fresh green chillies
a small bunch of coriander, chopped

In a comal or dry cast-iron frying pan, roast the whole tomatoes, onion, garlic and chillies (pricking these first so they don't explode) on the hob. The garlic and chillies will be roasted brown first, so set them aside whilst you wait for the tomato and onion to roast. When finished, de-seed the chillies and peel the tomatoes and put them in a blender with the onion, garlic and coriander. Blend till smooth. Season to taste and serve.

CEVICHE TACOS

A taco is a fried tortilla that has been wrapped around a filling, like an open-ended spring roll. This one has a filling of ceviche, raw fish that has been 'cooked' in lime juice, although for folk that don't like raw fish it has the benefit of also being cooked lightly in the taco.

It goes without saying that you should get the freshest fish possible for this. It tastes fabulous served with the green salsa and a salad.

Serves 6

250g wild salmon fillet, chopped into small, hazelnut-size pieces

250g sea bass fillet or other nice white fish, chopped into hazelnut-size pieces

250g raw prawns, chopped

juice of 2 limes

1 small onion, peeled and finely chopped

1 jalapeño chilli, de-seeded and finely chopped

a small bunch of coriander, chopped

1 tomato, peeled and finely chopped

½ tspn dried oregano

salt and black pepper to taste

sunflower oil

12 lightly baked tortillas (bought ones are fine)

Mix the raw fish with all the ingredients up to and including the seasoning. Leave this for about an hour, after which the white fish and prawns will appear cooked. At this point you could just serve it and forget the rest of the fannying about. However, this is a ceviche taco, so on we go.

While your oil is heating in a heavy-based frying pan, place 2 tablespoons of the ceviche in the middle of a tortilla and roll it up like a pancake. Put it in the pan with the overlapping side facing downward and hold it down with a spatula to stop it unravelling until it has sealed itself. Fry till golden (about 2 minutes), then turn it over and fry the other side till golden.

TORTILLA SOUP

This is an awesome soup, with the tortillas like super-croutons. And the lime is not just decorative: it gives it real life.

Serves 6

1 nice corn-fed chicken, jointed
3 litres water
1 medium onion, quartered
1 head of garlic, topped and tailed
a stick of celery
a sprig of thyme
$\frac{1}{2}$ tspn dried oregano
6 whole peppercorns
salt to taste

12 tortillas
sunflower oil
1 medium onion, peeled and finely chopped
3 cloves garlic, peeled and finely chopped
500g plum tomatoes, roughly chopped
salt and black pepper

to serve
lime wedges

Put the chicken in the water and chuck in the quartered onion, the garlic, celery, thyme, oregano, peppercorns and salt. Bring to the boil, cover and simmer for an hour or two.

Meanwhile, cut the tortillas into 1cm strips and shallow fry in the sunflower oil until crispy. Set aside. In a tablespoon of the oil, sweat the chopped onion and garlic till transparent.

After the chicken has been simmering for an hour or so, allow it to cool then strip the meat from the carcass and strain the broth, discarding the stewed-out veg and bones. Take a third of the meat and put it in a processor together with the tomatoes, the fried onion and garlic and a slurp of the stock. Process till smooth, add the purée to the broth and simmer for half an hour to allow the flavours to concentrate.

In a bowl, put a handful of the chicken meat, a handful of the crispy tortilla and top it up with the thickened broth. Squeeze some lime juice into the soup and garnish with the wedge.

MOLE PUEBLANO

Because there are so many ingredients, the skill in making this is to produce a unique flavour and not just mud. This one, arrived at after a fair bit of experimentation, is a good balance of sweet and sour. It is blacker than the devil's heart, and just as tasty. The most delicate part of the process is toasting the sesame seeds, which you must do with love and great care (indeed there is a romantic saying in Oaxaca, 'You are the sesame seeds in my mole'. I tried that down the pub and got a slap). Serve it with refried beans and the tomato rice. Any leftover sauce will keep well, and would be good with a pork chop or maybe a steak.

Right, let's get cracking on the culinary equivalent of *War and Peace*.

Serves 4

455g plum tomatoes

3 large cloves garlic

1 medium onion, halved

½ plantain or small banana, split lengthwise

1 apple (Granny Smith is good), halved and cored

3 chilcostle chillies

3 guajillo chillies

3 pasilla chillies

4 anchos negros chillies

1 chipotles chilli

3 cinnamon sticks or 1 giant Mexican one

1 tbs whole almonds

2 pecan halves

1 tbs raisins

3 black peppercorns

3 whole cloves

2 slices stale white bread, ripped into bits

100g sesame seeds, plus more to garnish

1 tortilla

2 tbs sunflower oil

½ tspn dried oregano

1 sprig thyme

75g good-quality (70% cocoa solids) chocolate, chopped

4 chicken portions

next door's caravan

a small West Highland terrier

a loofah

(OK, we're only joking about the little Westie.)

First, dry-roast the tomatoes, garlic and onion in a comal or cast-iron frying pan for about 20 minutes on the hob. Don't rush it; they need to catch and go a bit black, and the tomatoes need to roast through. Set them aside. Next dry-fry the halved apple and banana until golden, then set these aside. Dry-roast the chillies on both sides until blistered and set aside. Finally, roast the cinnamon, almonds, pecan halves, peppercorns and cloves for a couple of minutes and set them aside.

Now is the moment to preheat your oven to 180°C to roast the chicken portions (or you can poach them if you prefer). In 1.5 litres of boiling water, simmer the roasted tomatoes, onions and garlic. After 15 minutes add the fried apple and plantain, then, after another 5 minutes, add the toasted chillies. Simmer for 15 minutes, then add the roasted cinnamon, almonds, pecan halves, raisins, peppercorns, cloves and stale bread, and simmer everything for 10 minutes. Meanwhile, put your chicken pieces in to roast, then toast the sesame seeds in a dry pan for 1 minute and set aside. Next, set fire to the tortilla (yes, literally, until it is a black ember), then process or grind the carbonised tortilla with the sesame seeds and set aside.

Strain the contents of the saucepan, reserving the cooking liquid, and blend the tomato mixture until it is a fine paste. Heat the sunflower oil in a pan and fry off this paste, adding some of the reserved cooking liquid to give you the consistency of brown sauce.

Add the sesame seed-tortilla mix, the oregano and thyme and the chocolate, bit by bit, stirring until it is all dissolved. Then let the mole simmer very gently for about 20 minutes.

When all is done, pour the hot mole over the warm chicken and garnish with sesame seeds.

PRE-HISPANIC STEW

This is our take on a pre-Hispanic, Mayan dish. Traditionally it was made with rabbit, but we have found it excellent with pork, or you could use chicken. You should use dry corn, but that's the big-teeth corn, not readily available here, so soaked chickpeas work well instead. Serve it with tortillas, green rice and the hot chilli salsa. This one will stick to your ribs.

Serves 6

1kg pork shoulder, trimmed and diced	500g plum tomatoes
1 medium onion, peeled and sliced	4 garlic cloves, peeled
1 whole head of garlic with the top and bottom sliced off	2 whole cloves
5 bay leaves	4 black peppercorns
salt and freshly ground black pepper	250g dried pumpkin seeds
1.7 litres water or light chicken stock	250g dry corn, or 300g chickpeas, soaked overnight
4 chilcostle chillies	sunflower oil
4 guajillo chillies	2 yerba santa leaves or 1 tspn ground fennel seeds

In a large pan put the pork, onion, garlic bulb, bay leaves and seasoning, add the water and bring to the boil. Cover and simmer for about an hour, or until the pork is falling to bits. Remove the garlic bulb and discard.

Meanwhile, you can get on with the chilli bit. First you need to prepare yourself by putting on your extractor fan because the fumes given off by the chillies are a bit like CS riot gas. Then put your kettle on to boil. On your comel or dry cast-iron frying pan, toast the chillies on both sides until blistered. Put them in a bowl, cover with boiling water and leave to soak for 20 minutes. While they're softening, roast the tomatoes and the garlic until soft, then peel the tomatoes and set aside. Toast the cloves and peppercorns and set aside, and do the same with the dried pumpkin seeds. Finally, toast the corn or the soaked chickpeas till they start to go brown and catch, then set them aside to cool.

Drain the chillies, reserving some of the water, and put them in a blender with the tomatoes, garlic, cloves, pepper and some of the reserved water. Blend until it is the consistency of brown sauce, then pass through a sieve. Heat a tablespoon of sunflower oil in the frying pan and fry this tomato-chilli-spice mixture for about 15 minutes. While this is frying, coarsely grind the corn or chickpeas on the pulse setting of a blender and set aside. Then grind the pumpkin seeds to a powder. Add the tomato mix to the stew, then add the corn or chickpeas, the pumpkin seeds and the fennel or hierba santa. Cook until thickened and reduced – about 45 minutes. Adjust the seasoning before serving.

MEXICAN TOMATO RICE

This is a lovely light-red rice dish with fantastic dabs of colour from the peas and parsley. As well as the chicken mole, we also like this with something like a plain grilled Dover sole.

Serves 6

2 tbs sunflower oil
200g long-grain rice
¼ medium onion, peeled and finely chopped
2 garlic cloves, peeled and finely chopped

300g tomatoes, roughly chopped
675ml chicken stock
1 carrot, peeled and finely chopped
200g fresh garden peas [or frozen]
1 tbs parsley, chopped

Heat the oil in a pan and stir in the rice until it's all coated. Fry gently for a couple of minutes. Meanwhile, in a blender process the onion, garlic and tomatoes. Add this purée to the rice and stir until it is all absorbed – about 3 minutes. Add the stock, carrot, peas and parsley, and season to taste. Cover and simmer gently for about 10 minutes, until all the stock has been absorbed. (If you are using frozen peas, add them about 3 minutes before the rice is cooked.) Adjust the seasoning at the end.

GREEN RICE

Serves 6

2 jalapeño chillies
1 tbs butter
1 tbs sunflower oil
½ medium onion, peeled and finely chopped
400g long-grain rice
1 green bell pepper, de-seeded and sliced

a large bunch of coriander
3 garlic cloves, peeled and sliced
700ml chicken stock
salt and pepper to taste

to serve
lime wedges

Roast the jalapeño chillies on a comal or dry cast-iron frying pan on the hob, then de-seed, de-vein and set aside. Heat the oil and butter in the pan, sweat the onion for a few minutes, then add the rice and sauté for 2 minutes until just coloured.

In a processor, put the jalapeños, green pepper, coriander, garlic and a third of the stock, and blend till smooth. Add to the rice, simmer and stir until the liquid has been absorbed. Then add the rest of the stock and cover and simmer for about 10 minutes until all the liquid is absorbed. No peeping or stirring. Serve with the lime.

MEXICAN CHOCOLATE PUDDING,
With Mango and Lime Sauce

This is the best pudding we have ever tasted. We were taught how to make it by Susana Trilling, who owns the Seasons of My Heart cookery school in Oaxaca, Mexico. She serves it with a strawberry sauce, but we think the mango and lime is nicer! Try the blueberry and Drambuie if you have more of a sweet tooth.

The soaking part can be done overnight if you like. Make these in a dozen small coffee cups (make sure they are heat-resistant, not Granny's finest porcelain) or ramekins.

Serves 12

80g raisins
mezcal or tequila
200g stale white bread, diced
500g good-quality chocolate, chopped
2 tbs espresso coffee
3 large eggs
1 cup crème fraîche
110ml soured cream
50g caster sugar
½ tspn ground cinnamon
the lovely black seeds from 1 vanilla pod
butter for greasing cups

for the sauce
225ml mandarin juice

2 tbs caster sugar
2 mangos, halved and stoned
zest of 1 lime
2 tbs Cointreau

*alternative blueberry and
Drambuie sauce*
225ml mandarin juice
2 tbs caster sugar
500g blueberries
2 tbs Drambuie

to serve
whipped cream
grated chocolate

Put the raisins in a bowl, cover with the mezcal or tequila and leave to swell up (about an hour). Preheat the oven to 180°C, then toast the bread in it for about 10 minutes and set aside. Leave the oven on if you want to use the first method of cooking these. In a bowl resting over a saucepan of boiling water, melt the chocolate, then add the coffee. Turn off the heat but leave the bowl over the hot water to keep the mixture warm.

In a bowl, whisk together the eggs, the two creams, sugar, cinnamon and the vanilla seeds. Whisking continuously, add the warm chocolate-coffee mixture. Stir in the swollen raisins and the toasted bread cubes and leave the mixture to soak for about 2 hours (or overnight).

Grease the coffee cups or ramekins liberally with butter, then fill with the mixture up to ½ cm from their tops, and cover with foil. You can then cook these in two ways: as you would a crème brulée, in a bain-marie in the oven (this is easier for larger quantities), or in a steamer on the hob. So, for the first, place the cups in a roasting tin and add boiling water till it comes about a quarter of the way up the outside of the cups. Put the whole thing in the preheated oven and cook for 1 hour. Alternatively, place the cups in a steamer and steam on the hob for about 40 minutes.

Whilst they're cooking, make your sauce. In a pan, boil the mandarin juice with the sugar until it has reduced by half. Then, depending on which sauce you're doing, purée the mango or the blueberries and add to the reduced mandarin juice with either the lime zest and the Cointreau or just the Drambuie. It's that simple.

Turn the cooked puddings onto a plate. They should still be slightly sticky. Drizzle over the sauce and spoon some whipped cream and a little grated chocolate on the top.

INDEX

Huge thanks to

John Stroud and Vikram Jayanti, our producers and directors, who took the plunge with us, worked so hard to get the series made, shared in our adventures and kept faith in us. Lots of love to you both. What a ride!

Many, many thanks to our new friends at Penguin, especially to Camilla Stoddart, our editor: she's brilliant and glamorous too! Thanks to John Hamilton for his boundless creativity and enthusiasm, and to Chris Terry for his brilliant photographs. Thanks also to Tom Weldon, Becke Parker, Sarah Fraser, Sarah Hulbert, Eugenie Todd, Tiina Wastie and Chantal Gibbs for all being brilliant at what they do.

We give thanks to the film crew and production office people, who became a second family whilst we were on the road, and to Dave Rea, who directed four of the episodes and photographed them all so beautifully. To our lovely Belinda Morrison, the line producer, who did so much more and is just about the most capable person we have ever met. To David Keene, who was responsible for our sound – he has the patience of a saint. Thanks to Dave Depares and Dash Munding for their hard work and good humour. For keeping the home fires burning, thanks to Mike Snaith, our associate producer, and Anna Melin, our coordinator, for keeping everything on the straight and narrow. A big thank you to all our fixers and movers and shakers on location around the world who made it all much easier than it might have been. Thanks also to Anya Noakes, our publicist, for putting up with us – we love Anya's world.

To our agents, Maureen Vincent and Charles Walker, and all at PFD for their hard work. To Jed Leventhall, the legal eagle. To the lovely Marcus Mortimer, especially for his laugh, boom, boom, Basil!

DAVE: I would like to give thanks to the Roa Island Boat Club and the people of Roa Island. Special thanks to Sue Johnson for filling up my fridge ready for when I come home and for the best meat and potato pies going. Thanks to her husband Dave for teaching me to sail and for days flying. Thanks to my friends in Huntly, Aberdeenshire, where I lived for many years. Much love to Dr David Easton, his wife Jane and their family for being the best mates a person could have and always being there for me through thick and thin.

SI: I would like to thank my mother and late father for broadening my horizons and teaching me that anything is possible, no matter where you come from or live. And my amazing sister for teaching me to engage with the world I live in and to celebrate difference in others. Thanks to my big brother for his constant encouragement and total faith in everything I do. Thanks to all my mates for their love and support. All the coaches and youth section at Ryton Rugby Club for their kind words and constantly taking the piss. Douglas Hogg from Craster Village for sharing some of his vast knowledge of the sea.

There are so many people that we owe so much to and we are sorry if we have left anybody out. Thanks to all our friends and everyone who has helped this project either practically or with the enormous goodwill that we have had.

Ta very much, The Hairies. x x